# TASTE OR TABOO
## DIETARY CHOICES IN ANTIQUITY

To Anne

# TASTE OR TABOO

## DIETARY CHOICES IN ANTIQUITY

MICHAEL BEER

PROSPECT BOOKS

2010

First published in 2010 by Prospect Books,
Allaleigh House, Blackawton, Totnes, Devon TQ9 7DL.

BRITISH LIBRARY CATALOGUING IN PUBLICATION DATA:
A catalogue entry for this book is available from the British Library.

ISBN 978-1-903018-63-7

Typeset by Oliver Pawley and Tom Jaine.

Printed and bound in Great Britain by the Cromwell Press Group,
Trowbridge.

# CONTENTS

# ACKNOWLEDGEMENTS

The idea for this book was born from research for my doctoral thesis in classics that I undertook at the University of Exeter from 2004 to 2007. I owe an immense debt of gratitude to all those who took the trouble to glance at my work, offer helpful suggestions and moral support and who helped shape the material that eventually became the basis of this book. To Professor John Wilkins, whose sage advice and encyclopaedic knowledge of ancient food matters formed the basis of numerous hours of fascinating discussion (and often, much re-writing). To Professor Daniel Ogden, for encouragement and helpful words. To Pauline, Anna, Sharon, Steve and many others who offered constructive criticism and suggested useful avenues of research, and put up with my ramblings about Pliny the Elder and Athenaeus. To Tom Jaine and Prospect Books for making the creation of this book such a rewarding endeavour. And finally to Anne, for patience, tolerance and much sacrifice over the years, and without whom none of this would ever have come to pass.

MICHAEL BEER, EXETER,
FEBRUARY 2010

# INTRODUCTION

An influential and wealthy young man, whose prodigious physical appetites inevitably lead to weight gain, strives to keep excess flab at bay by repeated use of enemas and emetics. An elderly gentleman, also powerful and affluent and a close relative (in fact, the former's stepfather), has the disconcerting habit of having a feather put down his throat after his evening meal to induce vomiting, in a quest to purge his body of excess food and drink. Their wealth and status means they are afforded ample opportunity to indulge their every gastronomic fantasy. However, the former, with pretensions to an acting and singing career, knows that the public will not accept obesity in their idol (and it will be equally frowned upon by his peers), and that his over-indulgence is likely to ruin his voice and to impact upon his stamina to undertake arduous acting roles. The elderly man is merely greedy and wishes to make room in his stomach for his next debauch. In this rarefied world, where money is no object, go-betweens are able to procure whatever their employers require to satisfy their dietary (and other) peccadilloes. Meanwhile, the poorer sections of society (the majority) struggle to find even the most basic foodstuffs. The gap between the haves and have-nots is a yawning chasm.

I am, of course, not speaking of some rock star or scion of an old European banking family, nor am I referring to the food shortages that affect many parts of the world in the early years of the twenty-first century. The first man is Nero, ruler of the Roman empire between AD 54 and 68. The second is his stepfather and predecessor, the emperor Claudius. These anecdotes may seem to be derived from some Latin equivalent of the modern magazines which seek out and expose deviant celebrity behaviour, but are, in fact, culled from the pages of the imperial biographies of Gaius Suetonius Tranquillus, writing at the beginning of the second century AD, nearly a hundred years after their reigns. Suetonius wrote of the rulers of the Roman world from Julius Caesar to Domitian. He particularly enjoyed discussing the personal foibles of his subjects, especially their sexual and dietary habits. Such emphasis may just have been to excite his public (although how many would actually read or hear this material?) which had a voracious appetite for scandal, but there may also have been serious intent. Plutarch, a Greek writing at about the same time, also embarked upon a series of biographies. His aim was to write parallel lives of prominent Greek and Roman statesmen of the recent and remote past, accentuating the similarities between their personalities and the paths of their careers. In the introduction to his paired biographies of Alexander the Great and Julius Caesar, he states his belief that small personal details about a man's life may reveal as much as the great deeds of his public career.[1] The way that a man conducts himself with his family or in his private business and the way that he acts in office are symbiotically linked. In our own time, politicians may be judged untrustworthy if they have an extra-marital affair or committed some misdemeanour in their youth. Their desire for the private and public spheres to be treated separately will get little support.

It is not a new phenomenon: the emperor Tiberius, ruler of the Roman world between AD 14 and 37, by all accounts (well, at least by the accounts of Tacitus and Suetonius) was a man who lacked the common touch. Without the benefit of an effective public relations office, this old soldier was seen as aloof and cold. He succeeded a charismatic ruler (Augustus) who had a gift for political spin (the situation is not unknown in modern politics: think of Wilson and Callaghan, Blair and Brown). His disdain for the wearisome business of public life led him to periodically take himself out of the public eye and into seclusion (on the islands of Rhodes, and Capri, in the Bay of Naples). Such isolation inevitably led to speculation about what he got up to (not helped by the widespread resentment against the ruthless and cruel policies implemented in his absence by his right-hand man, Sejanus). Suetonius accused Tiberius of setting up a hotbed of sadistic cruelty and paedophilic abuse on Capri. This may or may not have been true, but it was felt that this was the kind of thing that this dour and lecherous man would do. The reputed activities of Tiberius took on the air of Chinese whispers or urban legend, a phenomenon still common in the world of celebrity gossip.

Suetonius was not above the odd bit of scandal himself. Employed by the emperor Hadrian as imperial secretary in charge of correspondence, he was

(1)        Plut. *Alex*. I.2–3.

abruptly dismissed in AD 122 for what a much later biography of Hadrian describes as over-familiarity with the empress Sabina.[2] This, of course, may be a euphemism for other sorts of naughtiness between scribe and empress; the evidence is not specific. The images of the emperors propagated by the likes of Suetonius – the homicidal Caligula, the paranoid Domitian, the tight-fisted Vespasian – have resonated down the centuries, spawning in turn a thriving industry to reassess the likes of Nero or Vitellius and, at least partially, to rehabilitate them in the eyes of the public. And yet, it is the image of Nero and Caligula painted by the ancient historians and biographers that live on in the popular imagination. It is this sort of tale of imperial excess that inspired the much later writer(s) of the *Augustan History* to relate the fantastical activities of emperors such as Elagabalus: if tales are to be believed, a Syrian youth who was a religious and culinary innovator, who liked to frighten his guests by releasing leopards while they were dining.[3] The salacious and exotic inevitably triumph over the dull and worthy. Tales of decadence and sensuality beat administrative and religious reforms hands down.

Drawing parallels between the ancient and modern world is a perilous endeavour. It would be ludicrous to suggest that we resemble our Greek and Roman antecedents in every way. There are many aspects of the ancient world that we would find alien. However, considering their vast legacy of art, philosophy, politics and science, it would be equally obtuse to say that no valid comparisons can be made. For instance, in my opening paragraph, I playfully suggested the similarities in the decadent behaviour of the rich in both ancient and modern societies. I also pointed out the enduring appeal of celebrity gossip and tales of grotesque behaviour amongst the rich and famous. The excess of the aristocracy contrasted with the miseries of the peasants is a common theme in European history; for example, the oft-repeated (although perhaps untrue, and certainly misleading) anecdote about Marie-Antoinette and her attitude to the culinary conundrums of the French peasantry. My examples concerning the behaviour of Nero and Claudius were also in the area of food, specifically over-indulgence and its subsequent ramifications. Again, the history of food consumption, and the often outlandish extremes of the dietary habits of the élite, are well-worn themes. If you were to ask anyone what they knew about the Roman empire, fairly quickly after gladiators would come a mention of outlandish dishes and people vomiting after meals in order

(2)    *SHA Hadr.* 11.3.
(3)    *SHA Heliogab.* 25.1.

to consume more (the Latin term *vomitorium*, understood by many to mean the room where this act was supposed to have taken place, actually means an exit from an amphitheatre).

I make the comparisons because, even two thousand years later, while much has changed in the way of the types of food that are consumed and the methods of food production, food is the biological thread that continues to connect the whole of humanity. Yet many of us have a very confused relationship with it. We agonize over levels of sugar, salt and fat in our diet. We obsess over calories, yet stuff our faces, hurling ourselves into an obesity crisis. How did we come to this point where food may be viewed simultaneously as lover and mortal enemy? It is only food, you might think: the fuel that stops us from keeling over and expiring. This phenomenon is nothing new. In some ways, we follow similar patterns of behaviour in relation to the meaning and ideology of food as the ancients.

It is not the presence of food that is the subject of this book, but its absence: not the excess of consumption but its restriction and how such ideologies played out in the ancient world. In the modern West, food has become a battleground. It has transcended its role as nutrition. Of course, food has always been more than mere fuel. Chefs ancient and modern have striven to promote their culinary creations into the realm of art. And food's role as a marker of identity and its cohesive power for communities has been acknowledged by authors such as Peter Garnsey and Mary Douglas.[4] Yet while many parts of the world live close to starvation, we in the West find ourselves in a paradoxical situation where wealth and status are characterized by extreme thinness, while the poor and the powerless are marked out by their obesity. Anorexics use calorific intake as a means of control in what they believe to be the chaotic maelstroms of their own lives, bulimics endure a continual cycle of binge and purge, wrecking their bodies, while millions of others, although not existing at these extreme peripheries, use calorie-controlled diets to fight against the physical reality of their appearance. I believe that some of these rather odd ideas about food can be traced back at least as far as the Greek and Roman world. Just as our landscape is littered with neo-classical buildings and the nomenclature of ancient government, so our mental landscape bears the remains of antique food ideologies.

In looking at some of the most powerful and strange instances of food avoidance in the ancient world, I hope to discover how such attitudes to food

(4)      Douglas (1966)(1984)(1987); Garnsey (1988)(1998)(1999).

helped shape the psyche, and how they may have influenced in turn our own attitudes. Did the ancients possess the concept of size zero? Did they equate weight with self-worth? Did they grow up with an ancient version of the 1970s advertising slogan for cream cakes: 'naughty but nice'? This last question is of particular importance (I believe they did, and it seems to have had something to do with fish) as its joky association of certain foods with sin is just a modern update of the way the ancients often associated greed for food with morally reprehensible behaviour. It is no mere coincidence that in many ancient texts one of the hallmarks of the evil ruler is a penchant for dietary excess. Dietary and moral excess are often synonymous. The obese are punished (and punish themselves) for weakness. The image of the fat and jolly extrovert conceals a tortured interior. However, first things first: let us define our terms.

****

By 'dietary restriction' I mean the practice of adopting a dietary regime that excludes specific foods or groups of foods. This could be for a variety of reasons: medical, philosophical, religious or moral. These restrictions can be voluntary or involuntary although, at times, those categories may blur and overlap. The phrase 'involuntary dietary restriction' is meant to indicate a process that derives not from social or religious legislation, but from external factors. This is less clear-cut than may be first supposed, as there is some considerable duplication between what may be thought human constructs and those deemed external elements. A primary factor could be labelled environmental: the constraints placed upon individuals and communities by landscape, location and climate. This geophysical dimension dramatically affects the type and quantity of crops and livestock available. Economic factors will also have an important role to play here. They will dictate the types of crops that may be cultivated, stored or sold, and will determine food production and storage based upon strategies for survival. Some groups or individuals may lack access to a varied assortment of goods due to their financial impotence. They do not possess the resources to acquire foods from beyond their locality, as costs of transportation and storage add to the price of items.

Dietary restriction is also provoked by the customs and behavioural modes of human societies. In these cases, I call it voluntary restriction. Conscious food choices manifest themselves in many spheres: in moral censure, relating to religious or cultural transgressions (perhaps of explicit taboos or tacitly acknowledged social codes); the control and curbing of dietary intake for philosophical or ideological motives; special regimens prescribed by medical practitioners for the prevention or cure of mental and physical ailments; special diets for certain professions or activities. It is arguable that some of these factors may be deemed to constitute instances of involuntary restriction: customs and cultural norms may exercise an overwhelming power over action. The weight of tradition or religious scruples may exercise an influence that overrides personal choice. In this instance, the line between voluntary and involuntary is obfuscated. Restriction could indicate the removal of certain foods from the diet, either temporarily or permanently, or indeed the complete absence of food altogether. Consideration of these matters will illuminate the critical role that food restriction played in the way certain ancient peoples constructed and maintained their sense of identity, both individual and communal.

It will also become evident that a dichotomy existed between the actual practice of dietary restriction and its ideological treatment in written texts. This is of course true in our own culture, where media obsession with thinness is in inverse proportion to public levels of obesity. Dietary restriction seems to provide a locus of concern for many Greek and Roman writers. The fact that these writers are themselves part of a wealthy male élite perhaps restricts the significance of their preoccupations. The female voice, so prominent in modern discussions of diet and body image, is absent from the ancient context. For those engaged in the daily struggle to obtain sufficient food to survive, such issues would surely have been entirely redundant. Wealth, however, brought both abundant food and the leisure in which to indulge in some ideological navel gazing. Greed, extravagance and alien foods become potent metaphors for the problems that were perceived to have arisen from social and economic transformation. Dietary restriction transcends its significance as a physical alimentary practice to become a useful way for the educated élite to voice concerns about racial, ethnic and religious identity and to criticize prevailing social norms. But such concerns could trickle down to the masses; the mocking of the powerful or the corrupt is often characterized in ancient Greek comedy by dietary greed. Nowadays, by contrast, the health and aesthetic issues surrounding food and bodily weight are a matter of discussion at all levels of society.

****

What prompts people to avoid food or impose limitations on their diet? In modern industrialized Western nations, the *raisons d'être* are diverse. One that springs to mind is the widespread preoccupation with body image, arguably one of the principal methods by which modern Westerners achieve self-definition. Portentous government warnings about increasing levels of both juvenile and adult obesity (with the attendant health risks) coupled with the recurrent presentation in the mass media of aspirational images of youthful, aesthetically-pleasing and affluent 'celebrities' have served to focus attention upon diet. A simultaneous longing to lose weight for enhanced health and increased longevity, a desire to eradicate feelings of insecurity and inadequacy about one's physical appearance and a yearning to emulate these celebrities has increased the popularity of regimes that seek to achieve dramatic weight loss through dieting.

These diets do not appear to promote a gradual, stable weight loss over a prolonged period. To ensure that the results of the regimen are not transitory they must be coupled with a programme of regular physical exercise. Instead, they endeavour to obtain rapid results for an often uncritical consumer base addicted to a 'quick-fix solution'. They are marketed with aggressive techniques – they often require costly dietary supplements – and are targeted at people whose previous attempts at weight loss have failed. The consumer may lack the patience or necessary levels of self-denial to await the results of a long-term programme of weight loss.

Many people that embark on such diets express the desire to reap the benefits of improved health that purport to be the ultimate goal of the dietary regime, but often place greater emphasis on the cosmetic and superficial results of the eating plans. They desire tangible, noticeable and, above all, immediate proof of the results of their efforts, even if the effect on physical health is, in fact, detrimental. Some of the diets that exclude certain groups of foods, or which require the increased consumption of other items, may give rise to some alarming side-effects. These may range from the merely unpleasant or inconvenient (constipation, lethargy, headaches, bad breath or flatulence) to the potentially hazardous (low blood pressure, blackouts).

In these diets, certain foods are regarded as being injurious to the self or at least to the objectives of the diet (rapid weight loss). This is not to say that these foods are harmful *per se*. Many nutritionists would deny that any particular food is detrimental, unless it contains toxins. The damage to health is done when a food is taken into the body in excess. Often these foods are filled with processed sugars or fats that are usually high in calories, but offer little long-term sustenance. They also tend to cause fluctuations in blood sugar level, which affects the body's energy supply and its ability to judge levels of hunger accurately. The foods are usually prohibited for the period of the diet, or, at the very least, rationed. Some nutritionists are sceptical as to the utility (or even safety) of these eating regimes, fearing that weight loss cannot be sustained (bodily weight may actually increase, owing to changes in the body's metabolic rates) when the specialist eating programme is abandoned.

There are, of course, many reasons why someone may wish to eschew certain foods. They may have, or believe themselves to have, extreme allergic reactions, which may imperil their health. Particular items may be prohibited if one subscribes to specified moral or religious codes such as those incumbent on Jews and Muslims; those who follow a vegetarian or vegan diet feel compelled to do so by a moral distaste for the killing of animals or for the methods of slaughter. Social and cultural mores often have a role to perform: some foods will be offensive to the community, or to elements within it. Peer pressure can preclude their inclusion in the diet. There are those who will think their position at the poorer end of the economic spectrum precludes them from purchasing some foods. Small incomes restrict choice. Occasionally, food scares impel sections of the population to exclude particular foods from their diet. Recent illustrations of this in the United Kingdom include concerns about salmonella in eggs in 1988, and the occurrence of BSE (Bovine Spongiform Encephalopathy), so-called 'mad cow disease', in the food chain

****

I mentioned earlier that there is always an element of risk in drawing comparisons between ancient and modern societies: distance in time renders them deceptive or worthless. An instance is the correlation between modern diets that demand the exclusion of individual foods and the desire of substantial portions of the population to realize speedy weight loss: there is little definitive evidence in Graeco-Roman culture to support the existence of such a phenomenon within that society, at least in the sense of the perception of a negative body image and a desire to achieve a similar body shape to that of celebrated public figures, in the belief that attainment will somehow facilitate the assimilation of other desirable personality traits. But scholars such as Simon Goldhill disagree, believing that the physical perfection represented in classical art, particularly in Greek sculptures, will have had an inevitable effect upon those who viewed them.[5] Such works of art may have fuelled concerns about body image or fostered an interest in diet, but this is certainly not evident from surviving texts. Latin writers, in fact, are rather scathing

(5)     Goldhill (2004), 11–28.

about forms of physical narcissism and gymnasium culture. Statesmen, soldiers or philosophers may have been viewed as venerable figures, possessing qualities that were judged laudable or worthy of emulation. Those merits did not apparently include defined muscle tone or a six-pack. The relationship between dietary intake and moral buffness is a rather different matter (more of which later).

Some of the other reasons I sketched for limitations to a person's diet in the modern world may be more pertinent to the assessment of this factor in antiquity, in particular the issue of food production. Modern man has distanced himself from his agrarian roots and has come to rely increasingly on elaborate technology and the ability to purchase his foodstuffs on the open market. The public cares little how its food reaches the dinner table so long as it pays the lowest price possible. Economic and physical separation from the production of food gives rise to a further step, this time towards intellectual alienation, even revulsion, when faced with its realities. The rise in vegetarianism is a reaction to this new siuation. This is a form of dietary restriction that allows the subject to define his identity by the foods rejected. A denial or refutation becomes an affirmative action rather than mere negation by default.

This book will look at a few of these areas of dietary restriction in antiquity and we shall see how ideas about restricted food intake and food taboos helped the ancients construct their own identities and the identities of others. I shall start by giving an outline of the general restrictions placed upon the diet of ordinary people in the Greek and Roman world. I shall then move on to some of the main types of food restriction and they way in which they manifested themselves. These include vegetarianism, taboos against the broad bean, fish, the Jewish food laws and control of wine. I shall also look at the way dietary excess was tackled by ancient lawmakers through sumptuary regulation. Finally, I shall examine the way in which the ancients often equated greed in culinary matters with moral depravity and, conversely, a sparse diet with virtue. We shall see examples of anorexia and bulimia. We shall see the corpulent and the emaciated, the deranged and the saintly. It is in these areas that food anxieties are at the forefront; it is here we shall see how anxiety over that sneaky extra fried dormouse or that third cup of wine impacted on the ancient psyche, and to see whether the dietary hang-ups of our Graeco-Roman antecedents have somehow shaped our society. Food restriction in antiquity taps into issues of gender, sexual and ethnic identity, religion and cultural envy.

I hope that this book brings (as it were) a fresh dish to the table. Welcome to the world of dietary restriction in antiquity.

CHAPTER ONE

# DIET IN THE ANCIENT WORLD

In order to address the issue of voluntary and involuntary dietary restriction in classical antiquity, it is first necessary to give some indication of the general nature of ancient diet. It is likely that for the majority of people it was one of substantial want.[1] Food would have been mostly scarce, owing to both economic and environmental factors. Concerns about what could be cultivated successfully (and about the dangers of disease and bad weather affecting livestock and crops) would have dictated the nature of diet for many people. Such concerns would have overwhelmingly influenced the way most people would have eaten. Our concern with the ideology of abstinence in the literary texts must be counterbalanced by an examination of its incidence as an involuntary actual practice.

In antiquity, we are able to trace the development of sizeable urban population centres, such as Rome, Athens and Alexandria. These vast sprawls acted as a natural magnet for immigration, attracting people both from inside and outside the Mediterranean region. There were also smaller cities and settlements ranging from small individual farms to larger towns and villages. In terms of food, the town was very much the consumer that sucked in most of the available resources to feed a ravenous and ever-growing population.[2] If the surrounding landscape was unable to cope with demand, then produce would be imported from abroad. This might give rise to a greater choice of food, but the prices would have put them out of the reach of many people.

The people were forced to eat what they could afford to buy or what they could grow themselves. We need to learn which foods could be grown with the

(1)     Garnsey (1988), (1998), (1999); Gallant (1991).
(2)     For links between town and country, see Garnsey (1988), 55. Compare this with similar modern stratagems; Douglas (1984).

expenditure of the minimum of resources (labour, time, money) and with the smallest amount of risk (the probability of crop failure, the likelihood of the crop being sufficient to feed the members of the social group, the possibility that enough excess could be produced either to warrant storage for future use or to sell at a profit).[3] Food production was structured around strategies of survival and risk limitation.[4]

Because of this one is unable to speak of a diet that was either consistent or homogenous across the Mediterranean region. The choice of crops depended on local conditions, both regional and extremely local – down to those micro-climates beloved of geographers and topographers.[5] The elder Pliny himself noted how the same crop may thrive or fail under differing conditions in all manner of territories.[6] It is difficult to talk of national cuisines, let alone international. The best we can hope is to make broad observations as to the types of crops and foods that may cut across regions and cultures, without delving into the intricacies of local or provincial gastronomy. As well as topo-graphical complexity, there is also linguistic confusion. The same plants or foods were known by different names. Ancient authors were not oblivious to this predicament, realizing the implications of regional etymological variations, and the potential problems for taxonomy.[7]

It is, however, important to stress the widespread, endemic state of hunger that existed for much of the time in much of the Greek and Roman world. This situation would have superseded (in many cases) instances of choice. The biological imperative of survival drove the nutritional impulses of a substantial section of ancient populations.[8]

In *De alimentorum facultatibus* (On the Properties of Foodstuffs), the physician Galen gives many examples of foods eaten by peasants in times of famine, such as bitter vetch, in happier times a cattle feed.[9] To circumvent shortage, food storage was of prime importance: crops were chosen on the basis of how long they survived.[10] Galen's observations on peasant diet are

(3)     Garnsey (1999), 140.
(4)     See Gallant (1991); Foxhall & Forbes (1995).
(5)     This idea has been explored at length by Sallares (1991) and by Horden and Purcell (2000).
(6)     Plin. *HN* XVII. iii. 31.
(7)     Plin. *HN* XVIII. xxvii. 105. See also Cubberley (1995), 55–68. Gal. *De al. fac.* 6.490 K (trans. Powell).
(8)     See Garnsey (1988), (1998), (1999).
(9)     Gal. *De al. fac.* 6. 546–547 K.
(10)    Garnsey (1999), 40.

refreshing because so many texts ignore the lives (and nutrition) of ordinary people. His inventory of foods, and the historian Peter Garnsey's work on the wider implications of food shortage, offer a vision of diet quite different from that proposed by other classical authors. Many of their pronouncements on diet, or upon the merits (or otherwise) of dietary restriction, reflect their unfamiliarity with even occasional food shortages.[11] Dietary restriction is often used as a metaphor for purity or virtue; a tool for self-improvement through self-discipline. Such concerns belong almost exclusively (in Graeco-Roman culture) to the educated and wealthy élite. Such pragmatic considerations should be borne in mind when considering their stance on dietary restrictions.

The majority of ancient peoples were compelled to survive on a limited number of staples. Evidence seems to suggest that the most important component of this diet was cereal. While it might be imprudent to make generalizations, the principal grain was barley in Greek territories, whereas there appears a marked preference within Roman culture for wheat. There were, of course, a number of regional variations. Beyond the einkorn and emmer discussed by Galen, other types of cereal included millet, rye, and oats.[12] Latin authors regarded barley as inferior, suitable only for use as animal fodder.[13] As if in confirmation, it was used as punishment for insubordination amongst the ranks of the Roman army.[14] But within Greek culture, barley was perfectly acceptable for making cakes, pastries and bread.

Superficially, this division of preference between barley in the east and wheat in the west seems founded either upon taste, or on some putative Roman desire to dissociate itself from what it viewed as an inferior culture, for the boundaries of taste were coterminous with linguistic borders. But more likely the difference lay in environmental circumstances than any cultural predilection. Barley requires little moisture in order to flourish and prospered in the parched landscape of much of the Greek mainland and the islands.[15] Wheat is far less suited to these conditions.[16] Barley is relatively cost-effective

(11)     Galen himself was part of this élite: 'We should bear in mind that he was talking about a world relatively unfamiliar to him and his audience, who were prosperous urban dwellers. For all his interest in the dietary habits of peasants (and there is no extant source to match him in this), he had no personal experience of life on the 'famine food'/'non-famine food' boundary', Garnsey (1999), 40.

(12)     Garnsey (1999), 15.

(13)     Plin. *HN* XVIII. xv. 75.

(14)     Suet. *Aug.* 24; Polyb. VI. 38. 2–4; Dio Cass. XLIX. 38.4.

(15)     Sallares (1991), 300.

(16)     Plin. *HN* XVIII. xx. 85.

and efficient in that it may be harvested sooner than wheat.[17] Such is the
desiccated nature of the landscape of both Attica and many of the islands
of the Cyclades and the Dodecanese that it was unable to support the food
requirements of much of the population; hence the need to import quantities
of wheat. Import costs would have added to the price of wheat and may have
pushed it beyond the reach of many. Barley was the less costly alternative.

Clearly there appears to be some divergence between the posturing of
the literary sources and the statistical evidence. Latin authors seem anxious
to construct an ideological fortress that separates them from the Greeks.
The demonization of barley appears to be one prop in this defence.[18] Even
Pliny's contention that wheat was the dominant and the superior grain may be
misleading.[19] His remarks may deceive those scholars who are not agricultural
specialists.[20] However, a closer examination of the texts reveal inconsistencies
in attitude and point to examples of self-contradiction. Even Pliny sees some
positive attributes of barley, praising its resistance to damage owing to its
early harvesting.[21] He also remarks on the fact that it has a long tradition of
providing food for humans, and notes that gladiators were known as eaters
of barley.[22] This is actually far from the denunciation it first appears to be;
it was meant to signify that it was a nutritious cereal for those engaged in
strenuous physical activity. It may also be ill-advised to take it for granted that
Pliny equates the longevity of the use of barley with a sense of primitiveness.
There is a suggestion that the long-standing use of a cereal lends it a legitimate
dignity. The Latin writers on agricultural matters such as the elder Cato, Varro
and Columella often see agriculture as being intimately connected to Roman
ethnic origins and harking back to a perceived golden age. The unadorned
rustic cuisine to which Pliny refers is ennobled, not debased, by its antiquity.
Opposition to barley often takes the form of a rhetorical stance; an ideological
bulwark against external dietary influence. However, it is also judged by Galen
to be nutritionally inferior to wheat.[23] It is a badge of Roman identity that
clearly equates cultural superiority with a rejection of barley.

(17)      Plin. *HN* XVII. iii. 31.
(18)      Galen makes a rather more dispassionate survey of both wheat and barley; *De al. fac.* 6.
          480–524 K.
(19)      Jasny (1942), 757.
(20)      Plin. *HN* XVIII. xxi. 94.
(21)      Plin. *HN* XVIII. xviii. 79
(22)      Plin. *HN* XVIII. xviii. 79.
(23)      Gal. *De al. fac.* 6.501–510 K.

Barley and wheat were by no means the only staples. Legumes and pulses were widely available. Legumes occupied a central position in the ancient Mediterranean diet.[24] Beans, chickpeas and lentils were but three examples; there were also others, including peas and kidney beans.[25] The status of legumes was ambiguous and, like bread, occupied a sort of half-way house between low and high status. They could form part of the *tragêmata,* the 'nibbles' that accompanied the drinking at a Greek *symposion* (drinking party) or could constitute an inexpensive fast food sold on the street or in the taverns and bars of a Roman town.[26] But for some, such as Ulpian, a guest in the *Deipnosophistae,* they were an indicator of poverty.[27]

Roman authors liked to use these basics as metaphors for an idealized historical past. They were used to symbolize the early republic; an epoch represented as a period of autochthonous abstemiousness and purity, with a concomitant rigid morality untainted by foreign influences. The elder Pliny attempts to prove etymologically the aristocratic lineage of agriculture by linking the names of a number of prominent patrician Roman families to those of various grains and pulses.[28] It has been estimated that it is the lentil that was the most commonly cited legume in Greek and Latin literature.[29] This particular pulse was favoured in the Near East.[30] In the *Deipnosophistae,* one of the guests, Cynulcus, remarks to a fellow diner on the ubiquity of the lentil in Alexandrian cuisine.[31] Chickpeas are another recurrently mentioned pulse. Pliny attempted to ennoble them with an illustrious ancestry, but in general other texts view them as peasant food.[32] Horace makes a reference to them as the food of the poor.[33]

It will be necessary also to make reference to beans, although they are a rather special case and I shall examine attitudes to them in much greater

(24)    Garnsey (1998), 243. Also Flint-Hamilton (1999), 371–385.
(25)    Columella *Rust.* II. vii. 1.
(26)    Mart. *Epig.* 1. 103; Faas (1994), 42.
(27)    Fr. 60 Olsen-Sens; Ath. *Deip* 101d.
(28)    Plin. *HN* XVIII.iii. 10.
(29)    Flint-Hamilton (1999), 375.
(30)    Garnsey (1998), 243. He cites the discovery of tablets at Murecine in the Bay of Naples, which reveal the importation of Egyptian lentils and chickpeas as well as grain.
(31)    Ath. *Deip.* 158d. Is this meant to be an observation on Alexandrian dietary patterns, or perhaps a calculated insult? Cynulcus may well be making reference to a common stereotype about Egyptian cuisine, rather than providing accurate data about gastronomic habits.
(32)    Flint-Hamilton (1999), 377.
(33)    Hor. *Ars. P.* 249.

detail at a later stage. At this point, suffice to say that they enjoyed a mixed reception. Pliny regarded them as the best of the pulses.[34] They could be eaten in a number of ways: raw, boiled or roasted, and could be used in soups or as an accompaniment to bread.[35] Galen notes that they too formed a common part of gladiatorial diet.[36] However, there existed a certain amount of hostility and suspicion of the bean among a number of groups. The Egyptians would not eat them, and their priests refused to even look at them.[37] They were also taboo for both the followers of Pythagoras and those involved with the rituals and practices of Orphism and the Eleusinian mysteries.[38]

The staples so far examined transcended hierarchical boundaries within Graeco-Roman society. They belonged exclusively neither to the impoverished nor the affluent. What separated the patrician from the plebeian was the way in which their foods were prepared and the context in which they were consumed. It is best to exercise caution when looking at the dietary practices in large cities such as Rome or Alexandria. Their size and populations make them special cases that do not necessarily represent the dietary patterns of other cities.

Fruit and vegetables naturally formed a part of the common ancient diet and, as with cereals and legumes, they could be enjoyed by the peasant and by the wealthy. Some, such as the nettle, were only reckoned famine foods.[39] Others, such as the turnip, were perhaps restricted (for instance by Columella) to country people or as fodder for animals.[40] Vegetables could be grown both in the country and in urban gardens.[41] Pliny thought that in his day vegetables were becoming too gentrified, attracting high prices.[42] An analogous situation may be said to exist today, where vegetables may be bought cheaply in a supermarket from the frozen section, or they may be organically grown and be purchased at a farmers' market. Fruits enjoyed a similar status, although Galen personally was wary of them.[43] Locally grown fruits enjoyed less prestige than the exotic and expensive produce imported

---

(34)      Plin. *HN* XVIII. xxx. 117.
(35)      Plin. *HN* XVIII. xxx. 117.
(36)      Gal. *De al. fac.* 6. 529 K (trans. Powell).
(37)      Hdt. 2.37.
(38)      These taboos will be examined in detail in the chapter concerning the bean taboo.
(39)      Gal. *De al. fac.* 6. 639 K (trans. Powell).
(40)      Columella *Rust.* II. x. 22.
(41)      Linderski (2001), 305–308; Lawson (1950), 97–105.
(42)      Plin. *HN* XIX. xix. 54.
(43)      Nutton (1995), 366–367.

from afar. Simultaneously, the enjoyment of foreign fruits could be viewed as a sign of decadence and luxury, which was contrasted with the apparent unpretentious virtues of the plain and the home-grown, *la cuisine du terroir*. The ultra-wealthy could have their pick of whichever foods they desired, no matter how rare, and cost would have been no object.

If today there is a tendency to romanticize and eulogize peasant cookery, for embodying a desirable lifestyle that rejects the impersonal rapidity of industrialized modernity, and embraces a more sedate pace of life, with an emphasis on the enjoyment of food as a sensual experience, to be savoured at leisure in the company of family and friends, this position was not mirrored in ancient texts.

Attention should be drawn to the special role played by two fruits: the olive and the grape. Their nutritional value was important,[44] though perhaps their symbolic worth is of greater interest. Olives were often eaten as an accompaniment to bread (perhaps mashed into a paste, in the manner of a modern *tapenade*) or eaten on their own.[45] The oil was used in cooking, in preference to animal fats, and as fuel for lamps. It formed an essential part of the bathing process, acting as a form of soap. Its value as a commodity was immense, transcending its role in the kitchen. Unfortunately, the appearance of the fruit on the tree was a biennial event.[46] The tree required little tending, but the farmer required foresight to ensure that at least four years-worth of oil was stored to guard against the ever-present threat of crop failure or the destruction of trees through natural catastrophe or acts of war. It would be reasonable to surmise that olives, too, enjoyed a variable reputation among consumers. Today, the finest extra-virgin olive oil (from the first pressing) can command enormous prices from connoisseurs, and serious gastronomes would not dream of using the same grade oil for cooking as for pouring over a salad. It seems entirely plausible that ancient consumers would have enjoyed differing grades of olive oil depending upon their willingness and ability to pay. What seems less credible is that there was any form of restriction upon the use or consumption of oil that was not connected with economic or geographical factors. There is no evidence for the voluntary shunning of the olive or olive oil in antiquity.

(44)    Gal. *de al. fac.* 6. 609 K; 6. 574–581 K.
(45)    Gal. *de al. fac.* 6. 609 K.
(46)    Varro *Rust.* I. lv. 3–4.

The grape is a somewhat different matter. It is, of course, central to the production of wine. The importance of wine to ancient Mediterranean culture cannot be emphasized enough. Its multiplicity of purposes included hydration, social lubricant and constituent of religious ritual.[47] It too could be an expensive possession of the moneyed clique at the summit of society or the default quotidian drink of the masses. A vintage wine savoured at an aristocratic banquet would have borne little resemblance to the vinegar-like concoction (*posca*) that toasted the successes and drowned the sorrows of Roman plebeians, soldiers or slaves. The principal difficulty was that wine was both hymned as an intoxicant, a necessary inspiration for both poetic and dramatic inspiration, and feared for its role in public and private disorder. I shall examine the way in which both Greeks and Romans attempted to reconcile this dualism, and will look at the way some groups sought to control and restrict its ingestion.

I shall also look to the role of dietary protein, particularly meat and fish. Both featured more prominently in the texts than fruit and vegetables, yet they formed a minor part of ancient diet. Not because sizeable sections of the population held strong objections to eating them, although vegetarianism (abstaining from meat or fish, or both) was an ideology of great interest to many writers – this fact is noteworthy in itself, it should be remembered that for a predominantly illiterate population (possessing perhaps only a very basic form of education, if indeed any at all), these esoteric literary debates were of negligible importance. Objections to flesh eating were rarely founded on moral principles (arguments for the welfare of animals).[48] After all, the potential 'rights' of animals held little sway in a society founded upon the wide and systematic exploitation and abuse of other humans in the form of slavery. If opposition arose against the consumption of meat or fish, it seems more likely derived from religious or intellectual arguments. Ultimately, a premeditated choice not to eat flesh would probably have been a dietary choice only for those prosperous enough not to have to survive upon a subsistence diet.

(47)    I use this term with a degree of caution. It may be suggested that the natural source of bodily hydration would have been water. However, if we posit a number of potential factors – the poor/non-taste of water, the possibility of disease carried from water sources, and a lack of knowledge concerning the diuretic properties of alcoholic beverages – then wine may have been a natural choice to slake one's thirst, especially if the wine/water ratio is weighted in favour of the water.

(48)    By this I mean widespread opinion, rather than ideological arguments presented by writers such as Plutarch . See Beer (2008), 96–109.

The relative absence of meat and fish from the average diet in the Graeco-Roman world was due to economic reasons. Even the lowliest farmer would have had at least a few domestic animals, most probably pigs. This was probably the main source of any meat eaten.[49] The prominence of pork may best be explained by the fact that whilst other animals were useful when alive for providing wool or milk, pigs were only suitable as a source of meat. They were also omnivorous, were particularly fertile and provided large litters. Almost every part of the carcass could be utilized as food and, once slaughtered, pickling, salting and drying ensured there was a supply of flesh for a long time afterwards.

The texts give a different view of meat-eating. Their focus is often the symbolic value of animal sacrifice in the context of both cult and state religion. And it would be unwise to attempt to extrapolate from the texts reliable statistical data or firm evidence of contemporary reality. For example, if one were to examine the dietetic details contained within the Homeric poems, the heroes appear to have survived (indeed thrived) upon a rather eccentric diet which consisted of large quantities of meat with no vegetables or fish.

Meat was eaten rarely, usually in the context of sacrifice as a part of religious ritual (at least in Greek culture): animals were slaughtered and the meat distributed to participants. I shall be looking at meat-eating and vegetarianism in much greater detail later. For now, it will suffice to note that a refusal to eat this meat may have been understood as an act of gross impiety, in effect signalling a withdrawal from a fully participatory role within the community: a voluntary act of alienation. Thus meat-eating was fused with the performance of civic and religious duty. Those who renounced it were making an explicit cultural statement (or at least were perceived as doing so). Meat was an uncommon and probably much anticipated treat.[50] Galen suggests that people were used to consuming a wide range of animal species. Besides the flesh of sheep, cows and pigs, he mentions donkeys, camels, bears, leopards, lions, panthers and dogs. Not all these animals are given his approval, but he does say they were a regular part of the diet for many people, who also ate many cuts, including hearts, lungs, brains and spinal cords. The elder Pliny notes that elephant meat was sometimes eaten, perhaps as a way of displaying discernment and advanced spending power: 'Luxury has given rise to fresh

(49)    Dalby (2003), 268–269: 'In classical times pigs were probably the commonest source of meat in most people's diet'. Also Wilkins and Hill (2006), 147–149.
(50)    Antiphanes fr. 225; Ath. *Deip.* 60c–d. 'Nobody eats thyme when meat is available, not even those who appear to be Pythagoreans'.

appreciation of the elephant – the taste of the horny trunk. In my opinion
this is because it is a bit like eating ivory.'[51] The squeamishness of the modern
palate (at least the Western one) appears to have been largely absent.

This brings us to the dietary role of fish. It may seem logical to conjecture
that it would have played a substantial part in the lives of people living around
the Mediterranean. Those who lived in the coastal territories would have been
able to use beach-based nets or boats to fish for themselves and their families.
Surplus catch could be pickled and salted to transport to those who lived at a
distance. The reality was a little more complicated. Scholars have contended
that fish enjoyed a status that simultaneously rendered it both a dubious and
untrustworthy food and an expensive and much sought-after commodity,
prized by affluent connoisseurs and gourmets.[52] Fish bore no resemblance
to man and existed in an antipathetic environment where man was able to
survive (submerged) no more than a few minutes. Fish, meanwhile, could
not live beyond their aquatic biosphere. Fish and shellfish did not constitute
part of the cultivatable *tableau* of livestock, items that marked man as a
civilized being. Fish and their fellow marine creatures needed to be hunted,
not farmed (although this situation did change in the Italian peninsula during
the late Roman republic).[53] The absence of fish from the tables of Homeric
heroes attracted comment from Plato, who thought fish inappropriate for
incorporation into a military diet.[54] Yet, within classical and Hellenistic Greek
literature, there are repeated references to the desirability of fish and shellfish
as luxury items, able to command exorbitant prices beyond the means of many
people.[55] Fish had become a symbol of status and prestige. Those who lacked
access to it may have felt themselves to be inferior to those who had it. And yet,
surely, shellfish could be freely collected along the shore by the very poorest.
Alternatively, eating fish may have been viewed as an indication of decadence
and self-gratification. The textual fragments of early Greek literature preserved
by later encyclopaedists such as Athenaeus are sometimes unclear as to whether
fish eating *per se* was morally ambivalent, or whether abhorrence was only felt
when appetite for seafood was indulged *in extremis*. A renunciation of fish
could be viewed as a symbolic rejection of the moral laxity and dissipation that

(51)     Gal. *De al. fac.* 6.664–665K. The quotation from Pliny is *NH* VIII.x.131.
(52)     For example, Purcell (1995), 32–49; Davidson (1995), 204–213; Davidson (1997b).
(53)     Columella *Rust.* XVIII. xvi–xvii; Cic. *Att.* I.20, I.19, II.9.
(54)     Pl. *Resp.* 404c.
(55)     Much of our information is derived from fragments of Athenian comedies preserved
         in the *Deipnosophistae* of Athenaeus; *Deip.* VII.

fish consumption could represent. I shall attempt to show that *les fruits de mer* precipitated a schism in Graeco-Roman cultural identity that went beyond the gulf between the affluent and those with shallow pockets and went to the heart of how man defined himself and his place in the universe.

This chapter has been only a *précis* of the most significant elements of ancient diet, to highlight the constraints already existing and a few of the problematic areas that need examination. It concentrates on the lands around the Mediterranean. A broader survey, taking in western and northern Europe, would uncover a different situation: where olive oil for cooking has been replaced by animal fats, wine has been supplanted by beer and there is a greater occurrence of meat. The geographical zone on which I concentrate points to a largely vegetarian diet, consisting of a cereal base, supplemented with fruits and nuts and with the occasional addition of fish or meat.

Food was a significant method of identifying and separating social groups.[56] It marked out divisions within society, and served to emphasize the gulf. Yet it was also, as Garnsey acknowledges, a means by which social groups cohered together, either through diet or through the manner in which food was prepared or consumed. The phenomenon of solitary eating is a relatively modern one. Ancient peoples would have mostly eaten collectively, in small or large groups, and to be a component of such an assembly would have been one way of signifying membership of a clan, tribe or association.[57] Garnsey's argument is compelling. However, I shall argue that an equally powerful case may be made for dietary restriction as a tool for defining self and acting as a badge of ethnic identity. Groups and individuals may be equally defined by the food they refuse. In a context where food is either very scarce, or where the purchase of unlimited or costly food is lauded, food refusal may make a dramatic and often counter-cultural statement. Food denial may have dramatic repercussions; it may arouse intense hostility from others, sometimes even persecution. It may isolate groups within society, but simultaneously bind them tightly together. Be it the advocates of vegetarianism, those who refused to eat the bean, the abstainers from wine or the devout Jew in the Diaspora, all found in dietary restriction a focus for the ideological foundations of identity. The ancient texts used these notions to explore the tensions existing within their own societies, and such issues as ethnicity, religion, class, even what it meant to be human itself.

(56)     Garnsey (1999), 7.
(57)     Ibid.

# CHAPTER TWO

# VEGETARIANISM

It seems plausible that most people in the Graeco-Roman lands on the shores of the Mediterranean lived predominantly on a diet of vegetables and fruit. By this I mean not a diet from which animal flesh had been deliberately omitted, but one in which meat or fish would have been a rare occurrence owing to relative scarcity and sometimes elevated price. The terms meat and fish should be used with a measure of caution, but I shall look at each separately, regarding them as distinct and separate categories.[1]

If meat was in short supply, it seems reasonable to suppose that opportunities to eat it were avidly anticipated, at least by most people. However, there were individuals or groups who actively chose to pursue a diet free from the flesh of animals, notably followers of Pythagoras and Porphyry. It is not clear whether they also objected to products which derived from animals

(1)      John Wilkins argues for the scholar to consider the separation between land and sea creatures in antiquity, as they each possess diverse and independent status: Wilkins (1993), 192. I am not sure whether the division is as bold and as clear-cut as Wilkins states. Puppies were sacrificed to Hecate; Plut. *Quaest. Rom.* LII; LXVIII (also for the sacrifice of dogs during the festival of the Lupercalia). Should one regard a hunting dog in antiquity as a wild or domesticated animal? It lives in close proximity to humans, so perhaps should not be regarded as wild. For Vernant, fish cannot be a part of the sacrificial ritual, as they are not a domestic animal: Vernant (1989), 37. See also Vernant (1991), 298–9: 'We know that in Greece wild beasts were not normally sacrificed. They were killed without scruple like enemies in the hunt. The meat, therefore, from this ritualized slaughter-sacrifice belongs exclusively to domestic species: pigs, goats, sheep and cattle'. On the other hand, Burkert sees importance in the area of biological difference: gods prefer large, warm-blooded animals: Burkert (1985), 59. If we accept Wilkins' categorization of marine life, then fish cannot be treated with meat as a single entity. They will need to be treated separately.

but didn't involve slaughter. Many modern foods have a substantial amount of additives, often of animal origin, demanding constant vigilance from the vegetarian. Animal-derived ancient additives included *garum*, a Roman sauce made from fermented fish innards.[2] Refusing this may have been particularly problematic as it was one of the principal methods of adding salt to foods. Honey may also have posed problems.[3]

Advocates of a vegetarian diet were a small cohort and were probably viewed as oddities or religious eccentrics, isolated, operating at the margins of society.[4] They may have even been regarded with suspicion and hostility, their beliefs perceived as a threat to established ideologies. Eating meat (and, by definition, not eating meat) had emotive connotations. The act of sacrifice to the god was integral to Graeco-Roman religion. This is not to say that the sacrificial offering always had to be an animal. Sometimes a beast was not available, or a choice was made to sacrifice some other item. Sometimes the rites of a particular god did not demand a blood sacrifice.[5] Pythagoras exhorted the women of Croton to sacrifice flat cakes, ground barley cakes and honeycombs in their religious rituals. He stipulated that the gods should not be honoured by slaughter and death.[6]

Animal sacrifice held immense symbolic importance, particularly for Greeks. The butchery of the animal and its division into offerings to the gods and what would be eaten by man made concrete the hierarchical triptych of god-man-animal. This ritual was a continual replaying and renewing of a covenant that existed between mortals and immortals.[7] A rejection of meat was, in effect, a gross act of impiety. Ancient religious ritual was a communal act in which men sought guidance or protection from the gods to ensure the continued survival and prosperity of the body politic (or at least protection from adversity and manifestations of divine malevolence). Dismissal of its significant ritual act (animal sacrifice) might be interpreted as a renunciation of the gods, even a betrayal of the whole community. Sacrificial rites were an essential method of ensuring group cohesion, with possible roots of the ritual

(2)    Dalby (2003), 341.
(3)    The exploitation of bees may not have been an issue if the honey were collected from the wild, rather than being the product of bee-keeping; Porph. *Abst*. I. 21. See Wilkins and Hill (2006), 160–161.
(4)    Osborne (1995), 222.
(5)    Iambl. *VP* 8.35. Iamblichus refers to the altar of Apollo on Delos 'which alone is unstained in blood'.
(6)    Iambl. *VP* 11.54. For Greek bloodless sacrifice, see Bruit (1983).
(7)    Hes. *Theog*. 535–565. Vernant in Detienne and Vernant (1989), 25.

lying in the practice of hunting.[8] Animal sacrifice involves the approxima-
tion of the wild in the domestic, and an expiation of a shared sense of shame
about animal slaughter.[9] The act of animal sacrifice is the crucible for forging
community bonds.[10]

In his natural animal state, man was thought a carnivore who, left to
his own devices, would eagerly satisfy his desire for meat. In terms of the
health benefits of eating meat, ancient thinkers were generally in favour. Few
objections were raised about meat *per se*, and exceptions concerned the flesh
of certain animals. Galen spends much time examining the species he knew
were eaten throughout the empire.[11] His objections to the consumption of
beasts such as camels and donkeys stem not only from questions of nutrition,
but also from morality. The meat of camel and ass affect not just the body
but the soul.[12]

There were others who believed man was not naturally carnivorous, that
consumption of animal protein was, in fact, an aberration from vegetarian
and fruitarian origins. To make sense of this, it is necessary to consider the
two diverse ways in which Greek mythology explained the genesis and
development of humanity. One exegesis regards the path of human history
as progress from brutish and primordial roots, the other as an inexorable slide
into degeneration from an idyllic state of bliss.[13] The first proposes that man
was originally compelled to forage for food to survive. His diet was limited
by his inability to utilize the flesh of animals by means of the transformative
process of cooking with fire. It firmly rejects the idea that man's digestive system
can process raw flesh.[14] For many in the ancient world, the consumption of
raw meat would have conjured up mental associations with soldiers under
siege conditions, forced by circumstance to eat almost anything. Alexander
the Great's troops in pursuit of Bessus had to eat the raw flesh of camels and

(8)     Burkert (1983), 35–48; (1985), 58.
(9)     Gould (1985), 18: 'Walter Burkert...has pointed out how much of sacrificial ritual makes
        sense only by assuming a deep-seated sense of anxiety over the taking of animal life'.
(10)    Burkert (1985), 58. See also Burkert (1983), 38 for the frequent rule that he who performs
        the sacrifice should abstain from eating.
(11)    Gal. *De al. fac.* 6.660–742 K.
(12)    Gal. *De al. fac.* 6.664 K.
(13)    Dombrowski (1984a), 19. Compare this with the Hesiodic version, where man originally
        feasts with the gods; *Op.* 109–126.
(14)    Hippoc. *De prisc. med.* 3.4. This is not entirely true. One may cite modern dishes such
        as beef carpaccio, steak tartare or sashimi to prove the contrary. Some nutritionists
        actually extol the virtues of a 'raw' diet.

pack animals.[15] Plutarch relates in his life of Brutus how shipwrecked sailors had to eat the sails and tackle of their ships.[16] It is Plutarch who makes the indigestibility of raw flesh for humans one of the foundations of his arguments against meat-eating. The inability to process a raw cadaver is combined with a lack of natural killing faculties such as sharp claws and teeth.[17] Man needs to alter the nature and structure of raw flesh before he is able (or willing) to consume it.[18]

The Promethean gift of fire presented mankind with the means to advance beyond these limitations. He was able to hunt, cook and eat meat. A crucial stage of man's development from primitive to civilized being – the discovery of fire – is intimately connected with the transformation of his diet from exclusively vegetarian to carnivorous. A comic fragment from *The Samothracians* of Athenion, preserved in Athenaeus, posits that primitive man existed in a state of cannibalism. The introduction of animal sacrifice and the subsequent roasting of the meat serves to lure man away from his diet of human flesh by offering something more appetizing in its place.[19]

Hesiod recounts an alternative history, where man is born into an utopia without pain or hardship.[20] The gods create and then destroy generations of men. Humanity is forced into a spiral of decline, becoming, as time passes, ever more distant from its simple origins. No longer is man able to pluck fruit freely from the trees. He must find other things to eat. Thus, here, humanity's degeneration is characterized (at least in part) by the adoption of a carnivorous diet. This type of myth in which human origins are linked with purity and simplicity, and an absence of hardship, is not unique to Greek culture.[21]

All this, of course, relates to the remote past: the foundation myths of Greek civilization; its creation by supernatural forces in distant times. The Romans, too, possessed their own myths. These were often, though not always, located within their own historical period, rather than some primeval era.[22] Romans liked to see their origins as peasant soldier/farmers, untainted by the corruption caused by the flow of wealth into the republic as Roman territories

(15)    Ael. *VH*.12. 37.
(16)    Plut. *Brut.* 47.
(17)    Plut. *De esu carn.* 994 F.
(18)    Plut. *De esu carn.* 995 B.
(19)    Fragment 1 Kassel and Austin; Ath. *Deip.* 660e–f.
(20)    Hes. *Op.* 109–120.
(21)    For Near Eastern predecessors of Hesiodic myth, see West (1969), 113–134.
(22)    Purcell (2003), 341. I feel Purcell perhaps makes too much of this, and I feel uncomfortable with his dismissal of the role of Roman myth-making.

rapidly expanded in the course of the second century BC. If the agricultural writers are to be believed, this was emphatically a culture that ate meat.[23] Latin myths of agricultural simplicity and purity eulogize a period when mankind is already making use of the flesh of animals. This is not to say that the Roman writers were averse to making reference to a mythical idyll at the very inception of their civilization, from which man degenerates.[24]

Of course, there is a significant element of Greek cultural tradition that eulogized the qualities of the aggressive carnivore. The heroic warrior-caste described by Homer in the *Iliad*, for instance, seem to exist on a proto-Atkins diet almost exclusively of meat. It is clear that realism was not intended (as a portrait either of the time of the poem's composition or the supposed time of the poem's events). It seems a literary construct designed to separate the élite from the common herd. Meat represents a form of elevated diet, perhaps closer to the gods than to man.[25]

Animals and humans enjoyed an uncertain relationship in antiquity, at least as revealed in surviving texts.[26] Authors such as Porphyry and Plutarch, who made earnest attempts to argue for the impartial and equitable treatment of non-human animals, stand out as relatively marginalized. Platonic thought envisaged a strict hierarchy of existence, with man at the top and the creatures of the sea at the bottom.[27] Across the Graeco-Roman world, animals were generally not afforded the same treatment as humans. They were seen either as being closely related to the manner in which deities revealed themselves to men (the transformation of god into animate form, sometimes in the guise of wild animals, at others in the form of a domestic animal, such as a bull), or as things to be used: for the transportation of people or objects, for the pushing and pulling of farmyard machinery, for food and for skins.[28] They were treated as functional utensils.[29] Wild animals could be slaughtered in the arena as entertainment. This was not just for visceral pleasure, but made manifest

(23)    Columella *Rust*. X. 1–3
(24)    Verg. *Aen*. 8. 315–318.
(25)    I shall discuss this further when I examine the role of fish (or lack of) in the diets of the Homeric heroes.
(26)    See Gilhus (2006).
(27)    Pl. *Ti*. 91d–92b; Gilhus (2006),86.
(28)    In Aristotle's view, it was acceptable for humans to hunt animals as the latter are by nature intended for use by humans; Arist. *Pol*. 1.8 1256b 15–26. Also Sorabji (1993), 116–119.
(29)    Despite being a work of fiction, one may imagine that the relentless physical beatings meted out to the central protagonist, Lucius, of Apuleius' *Metamorphoses*, transformed through a magic spell into an ass, was not untypical of the lot of the pack animal in antiquity.

the Roman construct of beast in submission to man.[30] A similar mentality is detected within Greek culture, particularly in the sphere of hunting.[31] Pitting one's wits against wild beasts could be viewed as a complementary activity to military training, sharpening instincts, reflexes and observational skills, as well as contributing to physical fitness and providing excitement and pleasure.[32]

Animals were sometimes held sacred, either being a god itself, or the terrestrial manifestation of some deity. The centre of animal worship was seen by the Greeks (as recounted by the historian Herodotus) to be Egypt.[33] Herodotus goes on to qualify this. Not all animals were regarded as sacred. He relates how humans mourned the death of dogs and cats, and how the death penalty was mandatory for those who killed an ibis or a hawk,[34] but he also draws to attention the ambiguous status of the crocodile.[35] It was worshipped in Thebes and at Lake Moeris, adorned with trinkets and tamed. When alive, they received special food; when they died, they were awarded lavish funerary rites and elaborate burial. However, in Elephantine they were hunted and eaten.[36] Hippopotami were sacred only in the province of Papremis and nowhere else.[37] Various animals that dwelt in the Nile were held in reverence, the river being hailed as a potent deity of fertility. Thus, Egyptians revered otters, the eel, the phoenix and various snakes and fish.[38]

The interesting point about these passages is not so much that they provide a snapshot of Egyptian social history, but that they offer a telling portrait of Greek cultural attitudes towards Egyptian religious practice.[39] Clement of Alexandria, writing more than five hundred years later than Herodotus, detects a continuity of attitude towards animals among Egyptians and much evidence of animal worship in his own time.[40] The Christian theologian, anxious to condemn pagan religious behaviour, is contemptuous of what

(30)    In the arena, man too could be placed in this submissive posture, as in the case of
        condemned criminals, slaves, prisoners-of-war or Christians.
(31)    Lonsdale (1979), 153.
(32)    Sorabji (1993), 172.
(33)    Hdt. II. 65. 2. See Gilhus (2006), 95–100.
(34)    Hdt. II. 66–67; 65.5
(35)    Hdt II. 69.1.
(36)    Hdt. II. 69.1–3.
(37)    Hdt. II. 71.
(38)    Hdt. II. 72.
(39)    Egypt is given as a particular example of a neighbouring culture which displays particular
        reverence for animals in a religious sense. One could also cite the Syrian attitude to fish;
        Lucian *Syr. D.*
(40)    Clem. Al. *Protr.* II.34.

he perceives a primitive and superstitious awe of animals. Yet, he accuses the Greeks, who viewed themselves as less credulous than the Egyptians, of similar gullibility.[41] Clement gives examples of how Greek communities worship, for instance ants and mice, as well as flies, doves and fishes.[42] This cultural similarity has intriguing implications for the vegetarian philosophy of Pythagoras. His biographers have maintained he spent time in Egypt studying esoteric doctrines.[43]

Some modern scholars see the marginalized remnants of archaic super-stition in the animal worship practised in Greece.[44] It is difficult to say with certainty whether these animals were believed to be gods *per se*, or merely terres-trial manifestations of divinities (who could adopt many different guises).[45] Many are the myths that tell of immortal beings that revealing themselves in animal form. These episodes were sometimes of rape and impregnation, the divine seed the progenitor of demigods and heroes.[46] Zeus was a prime example of a god who fathered offspring by lying with mortals. As a bull, he slept with Europa.[47] From this coupling came Minos, Rhadamanthys and Sarpedon. He appeared as a swan to Leda, fathering Helen and Polydeuces, and as a satyr to lie with Antiope.[48] His disguise was not always animal. To the imprisoned Danae, he appeared as a shower of gold.[49] To Callisto, he revealed himself in the likeness of Artemis.[50] He also impersonated mortals. He presented himself to Alcmene as her own husband Amphitryon.[51] This gift of transformation was occasionally bestowed upon mortals, for instance Periclymnus, eldest son of Neleus, king of Pylos, who, thanks to his grandfather Poseidon, was able to metamorphose into such beasts as birds, ants, bees and snakes.[52] Scenes of forcible intercourse between god and mortal were to become, mimetically,

(41)     Clem. Al. *Protr.*II.34.
(42)     Clem. Al. *Protr.*II.34.
(43)     Iambl. *VP* IV. 19. Much of what is related of the life of 'Pythagoras' must be treated as almost myth.
(44)     Renehan (1981), 257. Also Burkert (1985), 182–189.
(45)     See Gilhus (2006), particularly 78–92 on animal-human transformations, and 93–111 on animals in religion.
(46)     See Burkert (1985), 119–179.
(47)     Scholiast on Hom. *Il.* II. xii. 292. Also Apollod. *Bibl.* III.1.1. and J. G. Frazer's note (4) in Loeb edition (1921).
(48)     Apollod. *Bibl.* III.10.7; Ov. *Met.* 6.111. Also Burkert (1985), 128–129.
(49)     Apollod. *Bibl.* II.4.1.
(50)     Ov. *Met.* 2.428–9.
(51)     Hes. *Sc.* 35 ff.
(52)     Scholiast on Ap. Rhod. *Argon.* 1.156.

frequent staples of entertainment for spectators at the arena: the so-called 'fatal charades'.[53] The animals engaged in these mythical re-enactments were viewed differently by the spectators to those savaging condemned prisoners or fighting other beasts or humans. Their role in the mythical realm may have (briefly) elevated their status.

There was no homogeneous ancient ideology of what constituted the 'proper' way to treat or to conceptualize animals. It is likely that there was a rudimentary system of classification (a hierarchy) regarding the suitability of animals for sacrifice or slaughter.[54] Wilkins sees the selection as limited to domestic animals, but Parker sees a further subdivision, with a whole range that may or may not be eaten depending upon their 'social distance' from man.[55] And, just as there were differing and sometimes conflicting ideas about the correct way to treat and eat animals, so too there existed many diverse opinions as to why one should refrain from killing them.[56]

The pivotal figure when considering ancient vegetarianism is Pythagoras. The problem is that so much written about his life and teachings was composed hundreds of years after his death. Much is also highly contradictory and often constitutes nothing more than unsubstantiated rumour or blatant myth-making. There are no extant writings (it was claimed that he left none).[57] A great deal of our 'knowledge' of Pythagoras is derived from the biographies of Diogenes Laertius, Porphyry and Iamblichus, all writing in the third century AD. There are discrepancies in their texts as well as wild disagreement on some crucial points of fact. There is even confusion about his the exact identity. He appears to have shared his name with at least eight other significant individuals.[58] The greatest muddle arises from the fact that, despite his reputation for austerity and abstinence from animal flesh, some believed him to have passionately advocated its consumption for athletes.[59] Laertius does however admit that it is unlikely that Pythagoras the athletics trainer and Pythagoras the philosopher were the same person.[60]

(53)    Kyle (1998), 9; 54–55.
(54)    Wilkins (1993), 192.
(55)    Parker (1983), 363–364.
(56)    See Clark (2000), 8–15 for the arguments for vegetarianism advanced by Porphyry. Also Newmyer (2006) for discussions contained in Plutarch. Also Beer in Grumett and Muers (2008).
(57)    Diog. Laert. *Pythag.* VIII. 6. Diogenes Laertius refutes this claim, maintaining that he wrote tracts on education, constitutional affairs and nature.
(58)    Diog. Laert. *Pythag.* VIII. 46–47.
(59)    Diog. Laert. *Pythag.* VIII. 12.
(60)    Diog. Laert. *Pythag.* VIII. 13.

Pythagoras (*c.* 570–*c.* 495BC) was born on the island of Samos and moved later (perhaps after travelling the eastern Mediterranean, including Egypt) to the southern Italian city of Croton. His intellectual achievements (think the Pythagorean theorem) were considerable, although the lack of any surviving writings make his contributions a matter of debate. Certainly his influence on later Greek thought was immense, especially on Plato. For a time, at the end of the sixth century BC, he also had political impact. His religious beliefs depended on the formation of clubs or associations of like-minded disciples and they facilitated the control of Pythagoras and Pythagoreans over Croton thus bringing the philosophy and cult into the mainstream of politics in Magna Graecia. This settled expression of Pythagoreanism did not last long (the philosopher himself was expelled from Croton and died, perhaps, up the coast in Metapontum) but his influence lived on. Important elements of his thought included numerology (still surfacing in modern Europe through secret societies such as the Freemasons and the Rosicrucians), the transmigration of souls and the formation of cultic groups (with many links to Orphic or Cretan mysteries) with extensive rules of conduct which involved, in one way or another, abstinence or asceticism.

The biographies disagree over the exact nature of the Pythagorean meat prohibition.[61] Some say he abstained from all flesh, others that he renounced only certain animals, still others offer a form of hierarchical arrangement of acceptable meats.[62] Diogenes Laertius specifies fish abstention, specifically red mullet and *melanouros*.[63] He then says that it was reported that Pythagoras did, in fact, consent to animal sacrifice, but only cocks, young goats and sucking pigs, never lambs.[64] He also reports the opinion of Aristoxenus that Pythagoras only abstained from oxen and rams.[65] There may be a way to navigate through this mire of dietary perplexity. It may be possible to say that Pythagoras advocated a vegetarian diet not for all, but only for some. Porphyry seems to have thought that the ascetic Pythagoras and the athletic trainer were the same person, and sees no contradiction in this.[66] For his part,

(61)     See Dillon and Herschbell (1991) 6–14 for the Pythagorean biographical tradition.
(62)     Iambl. *VP* 68. See Clark (1989), 28–29.
(63)     Diog. Laert. *Pythag.* VIII. 19–21. Also Dillon and Herschbell (1991), 123, note 3.
(64)     Diog. Laert. *Pythag.* VIII. 19–21.
(65)     Diog. Laert. *Pythag.* VIII. 19–21. See Clark (1989), 98 for possible Aristoxenean bias: 'his preference appears to have been for an enlightened, intellectual P.'.
(66)     Porph. *Abst.* I. 26. 2–3. He mentions that some reports state that Pythagorean religious sacrifice did, in fact, involve the killing of animals. Laertius also refers to this; Diog. Laert. *Pythag.* VIII. 20.

Porphyry maintains that his own arguments in favour of vegetarianism are not to be applied to the population *in toto*, excluding specifically those involved in manual labour.[67] He is at pains to stress that a meat-free diet was unsuitable for those engaged in strenuous physical work, or in a life that requires them to be politically active.

The most plausible explanation is that Pythagoras divided his followers into two categories, committed to his dietary regime to lesser and greater degrees. This was dependent upon the level of penetration by the disciple into the Pythagorean mysteries.[68] The *akousmatikoi* were those who followed the teachings of Pythagoras but not hook, line and sinker. Perhaps we could think of them as 'lay' followers. They are contrasted with the *mathēmatikoi* who pursued a path of far greater self-denial. The lay adherents of the cult, who would have lived perhaps in the community at large amongst non-believers (a Pythagorean diaspora, if you will), were permitted to eat a limited amount of meat, as part of animal sacrifice (although perhaps were required to undergo periods of abstinence). The inner core, more firmly devoted to the Pythagorean ideal, living together in a closed community, followed a diet that was policed more rigorously. Porphyry, and the Pythagoras of Iamblichus' account, did not intend nor expect vegetarianism to become a universal standard, and they were willing to accept that it was not a credo to which all should aspire. Only one particular group was urged to absolute abstinence, those engaged in intellectual activities.[69] Diet is explicitly linked to its effects on the cognitive processes. There is a recognition here that dietary requirements may vary from individual to individual, depending on their needs. Meat is acceptable, even efficacious, for the physical life. The contemplative existence requires a different regimen and meat may prove positively deleterious.

The decision whether to eat meat or to abstain denoted group hierarchical identities. Vegetarianism was not an absolute but a way of marking the depth of commitment and adherence to Pythagorean ideals. In spite of certain views of Pythagoreans as monolithically vegetarian, it looks as if there was fragmentation within the group itself.[70] Porphyry, too, sees vegetarianism as

---

(67)    Porph. *Abst*. I. 27. 1. Clark notes the contrast between physical athletes and athletes of the soul; Clark (2000), 132, note 88.

(68)    Dombrowski (1984a); Iambl. *VP* 108–109. Also Clark (1989), 47.

(69)    Iambl. *VP* 68.

(70)    Such inconsistencies are picked up by a number of comic writers, as is made clear by a number of fragments in Book IV of the *Deipnosophistae* 161–162; Antiphanes fr. 63; 87;158; 133; Alexis fr. 201;223; Aristophon fr. 9.

a tool of demarcation, to separate the intellectuals and the philosophers from the workers and the 'doers'.[71] If meat is an obstacle to clear thought, there is an implicit criticism of those who do not 'think clearly'. The intellectual asserts his superiority. This categorization, inclusion and exclusion have been explored by the German historian Walter Burkert. He sees the Pythagorean precepts (vegetarianism is one, a bean taboo is another) as systems of differentiation and of control. They were not susceptible to logical justification, but were coded for comprehension by those initiated into the cult. He also believes that such precepts are analogous to those found in earlier and contemporary mystery cults. Diet, in Burkert's view, is a crucial element of identity, certainly for the Pythagoreans.

The Pythagorean refusal to eat animal flesh hinges primarily upon the concept of purity.[72] A rigorous and unflinching commitment to purity is combined with the belief that animal sacrifice violated religious sentiments, which included the belief in *metempsychosis*, the transmigration of souls from one body to another, including the possibility of a human soul inhabiting that of an animal. Pythagoreans also believed that eating meat was harmful to human health. It is key that the emphasis was on justifications that were beneficial to man, rather than to animals. One should refrain from killing animals not because it is cruel and unjust, but because one may be inadvertently harming a friend or relative. Indeed, one may be in a similar position at some point in the future, in which case a prohibition on killing animals would protect oneself.[73] An animal is a potential house for a human soul, and to harm an animal is akin to damaging a human being. In fact, it may be cannibalism.

It was not just Pythagoreans that objected to meat on grounds of health. Porphyry presented (in order to refute them) commonly held ideas about meat-eating being good for physical health.[74] Plutarch also deplored the effect meat has on the body, asserting that while it may fatten the body, it enfeebles the soul and intellect.[75] Appetite should be restrained as an act of will. Hunger

(71)  See page 42, note 92.
(72)  Detienne in Detienne and Vernant (1989), 5. Compare this with Jewish food laws.
(73)  Although this surely then is an argument for the *absolute* prohibition of animal killing, rather than just a code for a particular group.
(74)  Porph. *Abst.* 15. Also Clark (2000), 129–130, note 62. Note the importance of mental, as well as physical health.
(75)  Plut. *De esu carn.* 995 D–E. For a comic stereotype of gluttonous Boeotians, see Wilkins (2000), 98.

sharpens the mind and its satiation may serve to dull the wits. This view was echoed later by Clement of Alexandria.[76]

The ability of a restricted and meat-free diet to facilitate the cognitive processes has appeal to pagan and Christian traditions. The belief that the route to the divine is through the exercise of pure intellectual activity, unencumbered by the concerns of the body, is long-standing, and we may detect strains of it in such diverse thinkers as Plato, the Roman Stoics and Christian hermits.[77] Concerns with the affairs of the body were symptomatic of a growing feeling among certain philosophical schools of the untrustworthiness of sense perception. The senses diverted one's attention away from the realm of pure intellect, impeding its optimal functioning, and the beguiling temptations of bodily luxury were regarded as little more than a trap for the unwary that distracted from a contemplation of the divine.[78] Seneca saw a preoccupation with the training of the body as often inimical to mental well being. Simple exercise sufficed for the body and no more was deemed necessary.[79]

The argument ran that killing an animal was morally corrosive. It initiated a process that brutalized the soul of man. If one was willing to hurt or kill an animal, that person was more inclined to kill a person. Killing engenders killing, regardless of species.[80] It is precisely the point made by Plutarch.[81] By no means all in the ancient world believed killing to be wrong. The prevailing, dominant ideologies passionately espoused the military virtues and were

(76)   Clem. Al. *Protr. Beb.*

(77)   Pl. *Resp.* 372–373, where the 'body' of the state may become unhealthy through the ingestion of superfluous foods (including meat) by its citizens. For the views of Stoics such as Musonius Rufus and Seneca, see Wilkins and Hill (2006), 204–207. Clement of Alexandria urges the pious Christian to exercise restraint in food and drink; Clem. Al. *Protr. Beb.*

(78)   The development of ascetic thought, particularly in Christian communities in the east in the next few centuries, led not just to the assumption that the health of the soul took precedence over that of the body, but to the ultimate rejection of the body as a corrupt vessel whose sexual urges and impulses towards sensory pleasure chained man to an evil and depraved terrestrial existence and kept him from the bliss of heaven. Asceticism eventually leads to the horror of the mystics locked away in solitude, steeped in the extremes of bodily putrefaction and decay. See Vandereycken, W., van Deth, R. (1994); Grimm (1995), (1996).

(79)   Sen. *Ep.* XV.

(80)   The argument seems to run that the practice of killing sets up within the human soul a tendency to that activity.

(81)   Plut. *De esu carn.* 998 B–C. This passage has been used to suggest that Plutarch was influenced by Pythagorean doctrines; Newmyer refutes this; Newmyer (2006), 90–91.

suspicious of overt displays of militant pacifism. The defence of the state and the conquest of new territories were predicated on controlled violence and death.

The reasons so far offered for vegetarianism placed man at the centre of the discourse. Some authors at least recognized that there may be a justification that considered the rights and the interests of the animal. Plutarch made sustained and passionate pleas for the just and humane treatment of animals.[82] He sought to convince his audience that animals were far from the senseless creatures they were commonly portrayed. He was not, however, arguing against their use by man; some measure of animal husbandry was acceptable.[83] His arguments attempted to shock the reader out of his complacency. He talked of the shrieks and cries of animals begging not to be killed. Later, he spoke of the tortures inflicted upon animals to satisfy the appetites of gourmands. Some of the activities that he described may be alien to us: thrusting red-hot spits down the throats of pigs to emulsify the blood, jumping on the udders of pregnant sows to produce abortions. Others, such as force-feeding and housing in darkness, bring to mind modern methods of intensive factory farming.[84] Plutarch's views were prescient of modern campaigns against animal cruelty,[85] but they were certainly not part of the mainstream.

Ritual activities such as religious sacrifice enabled communities to achieve social cohesion. Rejection of them inevitably led to exclusion – political, social and religious. All well and good if this ostracism was seen as desirable. If vegetarianism was meant as an explicit statement of antagonism to traditional thought, a way of establishing a new identity that stood outside accepted ideological norms, this would not have been a problem. However, if hostility and suspicion from one's peer group was an unwanted consequence of a vegetarian diet, then identity itself would be called into question. The philosopher Seneca found himself facing such a quandary. If vegetarianism eventually became synonymous with Pythagoras and with a form of cranky asceticism that stood obstinately outside mainstream thought, it was also, in the eyes of Roman political authority, linked with foreign religious rites.

(82)    The principal works are contained within the *Moralia*: *De Sollertia Animalium* (*On the Cleverness of Animals*), *Bruta Animalia Ratione Uti* (*Beasts are Rational*) and *De Esu Carnum* (*The Eating of Flesh*). For a discussion of these works, see Beer (2008), Newmyer (2006).

(83)    Plut. *De soll. an.* 965B.

(84)    Plut. *De esu carn.* 994 E; II 996 F.

(85)    See Singer (1990).

Suetonius notes how Tiberius went as far as ordering the expulsion of all foreign cults from Rome.[86] In one of Seneca's letters, we find a discussion of a youthful passion for the teachings of Pythagoras.[87] He went as far as adopting a vegetarian diet, and he found it most congenial. However, this period of his life coincided with the Tiberian religious suppression, and vegetarianism was regarded as being a characteristic of foreign cults. In particular, it seemed to have been somehow conceived as integral to Jewish dietary laws.[88] He allows his father's fear of his being prosecuted to persuade him to renounce such a diet. Either Seneca's nerve failed him at the last moment, or he did not see vegetarianism as a particularly significant facet of his own philosophy.

Let us conclude this section by looking again at how vegetarianism had some potentially important implications for matters of identity. An individual or group could assume multiple identities. These may exist simultaneously. A Greek man was simultaneously Greek and Roman. Identity existed on both the micro and macro levels, and to a certain extent was fluid. Yet, for all this talk of fluidity, there were divisions and hierarchies in place in the Graeco-Roman world that were quite rigid. We may think of the Roman *cursus honorum*, ancient distinctions between the active and passive role in homosexual relationships, the separation between citizen and non-citizen, to be freeborn and to be a slave. The blurring or inversion of these boundaries could expose the fragility of constructed identities, inducing anxiety and threatening social stability. If one were to see ancient doctrines of vegetarianism in terms of similar anxieties about constructed identity and concepts of self-visualization, analogous currents may be discerned as being at play. The contemplation of the idea that animals should in some way receive consideration commensurate to that of humans in terms of rights to fair treatment (if not equal consideration) would have surely entailed a significant shift in both social attitudes and structures of political and economic power within societies. The issue hinges upon the question of marginality.[89] Animals are treated in a different way to human beings because, as may be argued by those in favour of meat-eating, they are not judged to experience as humans do. An animal on the receiving end of a physical blow makes noises and performs movements that, despite

(86)    Suet. *Tib*. 36.
(87)    Sen. *Ep*. CVIII.
(88)    Also see Cohen, 1–45 in Cohen and Frerichs (1993) for the confusion that often seems
         to have arisen about Jewish behaviour and identity in the Diaspora.
(89)    For discussion of Porphyry's use of this argument, see Dombrowski (1984b), 141–143.
         Also Singer (1990), 265.

being unintelligible to the human ear, may be interpreted as expressing some
form of distress.[90] However, some may take a Cartesian view and consider
that animals have no sense of anticipation: that is, the fear of impending pain
and possible death, regret for future plans unfulfilled, grief for one's parents
or offspring.[91]

If we concede that humans and animals possess differing levels of sentience,
we should also acknowledge that human beings may experience different
cognitive states.[92] I refer to those who are severely mentally disabled or new-
born infants. Some would say that a well-trained dog or horse displays signs
that it enjoys a richer cerebral existence than a small child or someone in a near
vegetative state. This argument implies that if sentience is a guide to treatment,
some animals should receive more consideration than some humans. In fact, in
the ancient world, it does appear that Plutarch was fighting for a cause that had
already in some senses been won. There did exist some parity of consideration
between humans and animals. Unfortunately, it involved downgrading some
humans to the level of animals, rather than elevating the latter up to the level
of the former. Those who experienced degrees of social exclusion (slaves,
foreigners) enjoyed a lowly status within the community, as did those who
were stigmatized and rejected as non-conformities. The crippled and deformed
were isolated figures, marked out as being cursed by the gods, and unwanted
infants (particularly girls) were exposed to die. Domestic livestock and beasts
trained for war could often be more valued, in terms of utility and aesthetics,
than the 'dregs' of humankind.

It seems doubtful that a conscious and deliberate vegetarian credo was
popular or widespread. It is likely that a significant role may be attributed
to external cultural influence in the evolution of vegetarian ideology. The
Pythagorean biographical tradition is hopelessly vague and confused and
cannot be relied upon to provide accurate detail of the genesis of Pythagorean
thought. It may be better to disregard the tales of the time the philosopher
was supposed to have spent in study in Egypt.[93] Nonetheless, the possibility
of cultural transmission from Egypt to the Greek territories may explain the
Pythagorean attitudes to religion, the sacredness of animals, as well as food
taboos such as those connected with beans. If Greek culture was not inclined

(90)    Plut. *De esu carn.* 994 E.
(91)    See Newmyer (2006), 66–75 for a discussion of this issue.
(92)    Arist. *Hist. An.* 588a ff; Newmyer (2006), 10–47.
(93)    Iambl. *VP* 19; Diog. Laert. *Pythag.* 3–4.

to acknowledge the possible source of these ideas, it may have been because of an amalgam of intellectual arrogance and unashamed xenophobia. The fact that those writing in imperial times were mainly writing in Greek invites the speculation that the authorities in Rome regarded this sort of dietary restriction as something peculiarly Greek. Its very foreignness immediately identified it as being slightly odd and untrustworthy.

To go beyond this hypothetical cycle of xenophobia, we may speculate that vegetarian ideas were banished into the intellectual wilderness for other reasons. Perhaps a rejection of meat was associated in people's minds with esoteric religions. Although eastern religions were to play an increasingly influential role in the spiritual life of the empire, those inclined to pay simple veneration to the *lares* and *penates*, or who offered prayers at the shrines of Jupiter or Apollo, may have shied away from the more extreme rituals of the cults of a Cybele.[94]

It is likely that thoughts about vegetarianism never entered the minds of the majority of the population. Unless religious taboos or legal sanctions prohibited it, it would seem strange if people who were forced to live on a subsistence diet through lack of resources, denied themselves from moral scruples a source of tasty and nutritious food.[95] Arguments for and against the eating of meat were between a small group of intellectuals who, by their own admission, saw it as an option for a limited number of people. However, if these ideas had received a wider airing, one may only conjecture as to how explosively revolutionary they may have been, and how they may have forced that society to indulge in an extended bout of self-reflection.

(94) The ritual castration of the male followers of Cybele, and the immersion in bull's blood that was known as the *taurobolium*; Catull. *Carmin.* 63; Burkert (1985), 177–179. Also Vermaseren (1977); Clark (2000), 122, note 9.
(95) Although perhaps one should consider the widespread poverty in the Indian subcontinent and the Hindu view of the inviolable nature of the cow.

CHAPTER THREE

# BEANS

There are many factors which make the taboo against the broad or fava
bean (*Vicia faba*) worth looking at in the wider context of dietary
restriction in antiquity. The obscurity shrouding the origins of the taboo
gave rise to diverse and contradictory hypotheses amongst ancient authors.
Aristotle, Cicero and Plutarch are among those who sought to explain this
bizarre custom. This ambiguity makes it an enticing topic. Recent studies in the
field of medicine may help cast a new light upon the restriction, transforming
what at first appears an obscure and small-scale dietary prohibition into a
phenomenon that could have been a matter of life and death for a sizeable
section of ancient communities.

The principal reason for the significance of the bean taboo is that pulses
must have formed a substantial part of ancient diet. Scholars such as John
Wilkins and Peter Garnsey point to factors that would have restricted the
amount of meat eaten: the importance of animal sacrifice in ancient religious
experience; the sheer economic waste of keeping livestock only to slaughter it.
Fish was also a rare and expensive luxury, beyond the pockets of many. Both
meat and fish were the subject of religious prohibitions. Egyptian priests had
precepts that prohibited them from eating fish, although this did not extend
to the whole population.[1] There are many references to the worship of the
Syrian goddess known variously as Derceto, Astarte and Atargatis, to whom
fish was sacred.[2] Lucian's *de Syria dea* deals extensively with the rites of this
cult of Atargatis. There is mention of the fish taboo, and he refers to a lake

(1)     Hooke (1961), 535; Plut. *De Is.. et Os.* 353C–D. Hdt. II.72.
(2)     See Burkert (1983), 204–207; Gilhus (2006), 93.

near her temple where fish were raised.[3] Severe punishments were threatened
to those who did not properly revere and care for the sacred fish.[4] As access
to meat or fish is restricted, the predominant source of dietary protein was
inevitably some form of legume or pulse.[5]

This was true for all social classes. The echoes of the *tragêmata* of a Greek
*symposion*, attested by Athenaeus,[6] or the street-food of a Roman town,[7] are
still to be found in the modern world. In supermarkets and delicatessens,
alongside potato crisps and various types of nuts, may be found dried and
salted chickpeas and broad beans. Pulses would undoubtedly have formed a
central ingredient of the diet of both the rural and urban poor.[8] A refusal to
eat beans may have had a significant impact on one's overall nutrition.

However, there were people who shunned broad beans. A bean taboo was
frequently identified as one of the essential traits of Pythagoreans, along with
physical characteristics such as untrimmed nails and flowing, unruly locks.
An aversion to beans became a significant element of the stock caricature of
this philosophical school.[9] Lucian talks of the typical Pythagorean in two
works.[10]

The roots of bean prohibition appear to have been in Egypt, certainly
this is the inference that we can draw from Herodotus' account.[11] Given
the biographical tradition that Pythagoras spent time in Egypt, some have
supposed the regulation to have been transported to the Greek-speaking
world by Pythagoras himself.[12] However, if the practice did originate in Egypt,
it seems more probable that it would have travelled by way of population
migration or trade connections rather than through the actions of one
individual in possession of nuggets of arcane wisdom. Also, one should not
discount the possibility that a prejudice concerning bean usage may have
existed over a geographically diverse area at the same time as, or even prior to
the report by Herodotus. Burkert considers the possible influences of Orphism

(3)     Lucian *Syr. D.* 45. There is also a reference in Xenophon to sacred fish, revered by the
        Syrians in the Chalus river; Xen. *An.* 1.4.9.
(4)     Plut. *De superst.* 170D.
(5)     Columella *Rust.* II. vii; Garnsey (1998), 243.
(6)     Ath. *Deip.* II 54f; IV 138a (quoting Pl. *Resp.* 372c); IV, 139a.
(7)     Mart. *Epi.* 1.103.
(8)     Garnsey (1998), 219.
(9)     Burkert (1972), 183.
(10)    Lucian *Somn.; Vit. auct.*
(11)    Hdt. II 37; Plut. *Quaest. conviv.* VIII.8.279; Gorman (1979), 22.
(12)    Iambl. *VP* 19; Diog. Laert. *Pythag.* 3–4.

upon Pythagorean ideology.[13] Pausanias relates the tale that Demeter (the goddess of agriculture) presented the Pheneatians (inhabitants of the city of Pheneos near Corinth) with a number of legumes, but specifically excluded the broad bean.[14] Hence, the broad bean was one of the items of food that were regarded as unacceptable to initiates into the Eleusinian mysteries. This cult demanded a series of temporary fasts and abstinences.[15] Burkert cites other initiatory requirements for Greek mystery cults. They include dietary restrictions, the wearing (or avoidance) of particular items of clothing, and sexual tests and obligations. These appear to perform a purificatory function.[16] Burkert considers the possibility of the widespread occurrence of similar cultic rituals among different sects.[17]

If Burkert is correct, the Pythagorean rules were not an innovation, but comparable to those in place in other mystery cults.[18] They codified a pre-existing folk tradition. Burkert asserts that such practices supplied not only a means of binding together members of the group and excluding non-members, but were used to enforce control and to strengthen the position of the priestly leaders. If this model is correct, then the bean prohibition, whether based on fear and reverence of, or disgust for the legume, may be interpreted as a technique designed to strengthen systems of control and manipulation within the Pythagorean community, marking out the leader as a special individual, worthy of fealty.

It is perhaps worth considering the precise wording of the bean taboo as it has been transmitted. Empedocles and Callimachus, who were both cited by Aulus Gellius, used almost identical phrases for the maxim.[19] The fragment of Callimachus reads as follows:

And withhold your hands from beans, a harmful food, I say, as Pythagoras ordered.[20]

(13)    For the possible influences of Orphism upon Pythagorean ideology, see Burkert (1972), 125–133.
(14)    Pausanias. 8.15.3; Flint-Hamilton (1999), 379.
(15)    Burkert (1972), 177; Porphyry *Abst.* 4. 16: '[to abstain from] fish and beans and pomegranates and apples, and one who has contact with the marriage bed is equally polluted with those who have died'. Also Grmek (1983), 214. Similar restrictions were in place for another festival of Demeter, the Haloa; 358–363.
(16)    Burkert (1972), 177–178.
(17)    Burkert (1972), 178.
(18)    See Burkert (1985), 276–304, in particular Eleusis; 285–290. Parker (1983); 358–363.
(19)    Gell. *NA.* IV xi, 2; 9.
(20)    Fr. 128, Sch; Gell. *NA.* IV xi, 2

Empedocles, named by Gellius as an adherent of Pythagoras, is quoted thus:

> Wretches, utter wretches, withhold your hands from beans. [21]

Ancient sources tended to divide into three camps on the matter of beans. The first saw the taboo as a technique that sought to facilitate the achievement of a state of purity. The next saw in the prohibition an allegorical message, a code designed to be tacitly understood to prevent other forms of behaviour. The third held the bean as a source of potential physiological and psychic disturbance. [22] In the Pythagorean biographical tradition, Iamblichus discussed some of the reasons that Pythagoreans eliminated specified foods from their diet: because they had unfortunate physical effects (flatulence, a distended stomach, drowsiness), or were deemed in some way sacred. [23]

This refusal to engage with beans appears to have extended far beyond questions of diet and cookery. Iamblichus told of an attempt by the fourth-century BC Syracusan tyrant Dionysius to apprehend certain followers of Pythagoras. He despatched his general Eurymenes to effect a capture:

> Therefore in Phalae, a rugged part of Tarentum, through which the Pythagoreans were scheduled to pass, Eurymenes insidiously concealed his troop; and when the unsuspecting Pythagoreans reached there about noon, the soldiers rushed upon them with shouts, after the manner of robbers. Disturbed and terrified at an attack so unexpected, at the superior number of their enemies, – the Pythagoreans amounting to no more than ten, – and being unarmed against regularly equipped soldiery, the Pythagoreans saw that they would inevitably be taken captive, so they decided that their only safety lay in flight, which they did not consider inadmissible to virtue. For they knew that according to right reason, fortitude is the art of avoiding as well as enduring. So they would have escaped, and their pursuit would have been given up by Eurymenes' soldiers, who were heavily armed, had their flight not led them up against a field sown with beans, which were already flowering.

(21)    Fr. 141, Diehls; Gell. *NA*. IV xi, 9.
(22)    Iambl. *VP* 24.106; Diog. Laert. *Pythag.* 8.24; Cic. *Div*. I. xxix. 62–63
(23)    Iambl. *VP* 24.106 See Clark (1989), 24, note 61.

Unwilling to violate their principle not to touch beans, they
stood still, and driven to desperation turned, and attacked their
pursuers with stones and sticks, and whatever they found to hand, till
they had wounded many, and slain some. But (numbers told), and all
the Pythagoreans were slain by the spearmen, as none of them would
suffer himself to be taken captive, preferring death, according to the
Pythagorean teachings.

In this context, Iamblichus chose to use the word 'touch', rather than anything
associated with eating.[24]

Diogenes Laertius offered up two possible justifications for the taboo.
Firstly, the physical effects of flatulence and stomach upsets,[25] later, that
beans were one of a selection of foods that were taboo in order to achieve a
state of ritual purity.[26] Seeking to achieve clarification, he invoked Aristotle's
reasons for the prohibition. However, far from illuminating the problem, they
only muddy the water. Aristotle suggested they resembled male genitals (the
testicles), that they have 'a harmful nature', that they somehow have links with
oligarchy and, in cryptic (and incomprehensible) summation, 'they are like
the nature of the whole'.[27] It appears Aristotle had no clear notion as to why
this dietary rule existed.[28] His hypotheses attempted to cover all areas and do
not sit particularly well together. The linking of beans with oligarchy seems
to indicate that Aristotle believed the bean taboo was, for Pythagoreans, a
symbolic rejection of conventional political systems (in which beans were used
as ballots in elections). He seems unsure whether the hostility was directed
towards the bean per se or at some other entity, of which the bean was symbolic
embodiment.[29]

Plutarch seems to have inclined towards the conjecture that the Pythagorean imperative originated from Egypt.[30] Cicero, however, thought the
custom linked to the physical effects of the bean: flatulence has a disruptive

(24)    Iambl. *VP* 31.191.
(25)    Diog. Laert. *Pythag.* 8.24.
(26)    Diog. Laert. *Pythag.* 8.33–34.
(27)    Diog. Laert. *Pythag.* 8.34.
(28)    See Burkert (1972), 183–184.
(29)    For Aristotle on Pythagoreanism, see Philip (1963a), 251–265; (1963b), 185–198.
(30)    Plut. *Quaest. conviv.* VIII.8.729. It seems that Plutarch was of the opinion that there
        may have existed other taboos concerning the bean, beyond its Egyptian influence, as
        elsewhere he asserts that abstention from legumes is a generic characteristic of all those
        occupying holy office; Plut. *Quaest. Rom.* 95.

effect upon sleep patterns and may be the source of neurological disturbance and hence unusual dreams. In this, he is in accord with Diogenes Laertius.[31]

In all probability, it would be unwise to suppose that the prohibition of beans had uniform characteristics across the Mediterranean world. Latin agricultural authors such as the elder Cato, Varro and Columella all related techniques of planting and harvesting the bean, which seems to imply that a taboo was not prevalent within their culture.[32] Galen, while acknowledging the flatulence, nonetheless praised the bean as nutritious and versatile, extensively used.[33] He notes that it was a regular feature of the diet of gladiators.[34] He also claimed that bean flour could act as an exfoliant and was effective in removing dirt from the skin.[35] He fails to mention any prohibition or taboo concerning the bean, and since he must have been aware of the custom, evidently felt it was of little importance or relevance (certainly from a medical viewpoint).

The elder Pliny was even more unstinting in his praise of this legume, drawing attention to its wide range of uses, including its addition to bread flour.[36] He did address himself to the issue of the Pythagorean rule, associating it with potential somatic disorders, particularly insomnia.[37] As with Aristotle, Pliny suggested other possible reasons, including the linking of beans with religious custom and its qualities as a talisman that could bring good fortune in the auction place.[38] Reverence for, or avoidance of, the bean was present not just within the confines of an esoteric doctrine, but within folklore and popular superstition.

Although all these varied opinions are voiced, they do seem at one in suggesting that there existed reservations about the broad bean, both at the level of folk wisdom and within the more restricted environs of quasi-mystical religious and political groups. However, even here there was much disagreement. Aulus Gellius, whilst duly recording the opinions of Callimachus and Empedocles, asserts that Aristoxenus, a pupil of Aristotle, believed that, far from being excluded from the diet, beans were, in fact, a

(31)    Cic. *Div*. I. xxix. 62–63; Diog. Laert. *Pythag* 8.24. Kingsley (1995), 285.
(32)    Cato *Agr*. XXXV.1; XXXVI.2; Varro *Rust*. XXXII.2; Collumella *Rust*. II.vii.
(33)    Dioscor. *De mat. Med*. 2.127, who also commented upon its impact upon the dreaming process.
(34)    Gal. *De al. fac*. 6.529 K.
(35)    Gal. *De al. fac*. 6.530 K. For beans and pulses employed as beauty aids in antiquity, see Green (1979), 381–392.
(36)    Plin. *HN* XVIII.xxx.117.
(37)    Plin. *HN* XVIII.xxx.118.
(38)    Plin. *HN* XVIII.xxx.119.

particular Pythagorean favourite.[39] Given that this runs counter to the general consensus (at least according to the extant material), some doubt has been cast on this Aristoxenian explanation.[40]

In addition, Gellius suggests that the misunderstanding is etymological. He maintained that people had misinterpreted the Empedoclean line, and that *kuamos* (bean) was in fact a synonym for testicles.[41] With this linguistic interpretation, the exhortation is to sexual, not dietary, abstinence. Plutarch also saw a connection with sex, attempting to link the flatulent qualities of beans with sexual desire.[42] Such a view presumes that the Pythagorean precepts should be understood as symbolic and allegorical. Gellius' interpretation of Empedocles seems compelling, and the modern critic Walter Burkert has posited that the word *kuamos* has other connotations that would tend to endorse this hypothesis.[43]

It could be argued that one of the principal functions of food prohibitions was to simplify diet.[44] Foods that are viewed as 'luxurious' may be discarded by the individual or community committed to a spiritual existence.[45] Learning to survive on basic foodstuffs could be an act of self-discipline and a rejection of the perceived frivolities of corporeal existence. However, this surely cannot apply to the broad bean, whose ubiquity and lowly status hardly made it a sybaritic delicacy. Rejection of the broad bean cannot have implied a rejection of luxury.[46] Those who may have viewed the Pythagorean community as a hermetically sealed patrician clique would surely have had their worst fears confirmed by the rejection of a staple food of the impoverished majority.

It seems too simple to dismiss the precept as a marker of social identity that was chosen arbitrarily. It may have been used as a way of forging and maintaining social cohesion; a pivot around which to stabilize the group identity in the face of a hostile or uncomprehending wider world. Yet this may be only half of the story. The evidence points to greater symbolic weight attached

(39)    Gell. *NA*. IV.ii.4–5.
(40)    I am grateful to Dr Peter van Nuffelen for pointing out the possible anti-Pythagorean stance of Aristoxenus. See Burkert (1972), 106–108 for Aristoxenus on Pythagoreanism.
(41)    The association is derived from the verb *kuein*, 'to conceive', or, 'to impregnate'
(42)    Plut. *Quaest. Rom.* 95.
(43)    Burkert (1972), 176.
(44)    Diog. Laert. *Pythag.* 8.13.
(45)    Wilkins and Hill (2006), 195; 204–207 for advocates of dietary restriction for the philosopher: for example, Musonius Rufus, Seneca, Plato.
(46)    If anything, it seems to demonstrate a spurning of the food of the penurious peasantry.

to the broad bean by both Greeks and Romans (and other cultures, such as
the Egyptians). The religious and cultural baggage surrounding this legume
appears less apparent within Latin culture. Perhaps this is because we possess
Latin texts that tend to assess the agricultural and nutritional value of the
bean, rather than focusing upon its symbolic resonances. This in turn may
be a Roman rejection of Greek practices, although this is unlikely. Clearly
there existed a reverence for the potential supernatural qualities of the bean
in Latin culture. The preponderance of material concerning the bean taboo
in Greek texts may simply be an historical accident of survival. However it is
not impossible that the imbalance between the two cultures concerning this
particular legume may be explained by the way in which certain sections of
ancient populations physically reacted to the broad bean.

   Latin writers did investigate the mysteries of the taboo, but with an almost
antiquarian interest. It was a problem upon which to exert the intellect and
an enigma to be solved. Nevertheless, in certain contexts (mainly religious)
a certain veneration surrounded the bean. This was not always manifested as
avoidance; sometimes it was seen to act as a charm, or as an integral element
of specific rituals and festivals, such as the Lemuria – when Romans exorcized
ghosts and evil spirits from their homes (*lemures* are restless spirits). The spirits
were propitiated with offerings of beans. It was certainly associated with death,
and perhaps served as a marker not merely to separate and segregate social
groups and individuals, as may have been the case with both the Pythagoreans
and some mystery cults, but the boundaries between life and death. Beans may
even have been viewed as a form of *memento mori*, a concrete reminder of
human mortality. What both cultures appear to have shared was a sentiment
that linked the bean with the souls of the dead. One of the reasons advanced
by Plutarch (he offers up several) is that a bean prohibition may have been
intimately linked with their use in sepulchral ritual.[47] The Pythagorean
belief in *metempsychosis*, the transmigration of souls, meant that if beans
potentially contained life, then consuming them was as much a transgression
for Pythagoreans as the ingestion of animal flesh. It may have, taken to its
logical extreme, been assumed to have been equivalent to cannibalism. The
bean was clearly held to possess a supernatural link with death and decay,

(47)   Plut. *Quaest. Rom.* 95. The elder Pliny notes a similar attitude: 'Varro et ob haec flaminem
       ea non vesci tradit et quoniam in flore eius litterae lugubres reperiantur': 'Varro relates
       that it is both for this reason that the priest does not eat it and because in its flower are
       discovered letters of mourning' (Plin. *NH.* XVIII.xxx.119).

and this ensured that it was treated with reverence and respect, or fearfully avoided (at least by some).

There may be another, and simpler, explanation for the association of the broad bean and death: beans might kill. Legumes are not innocuous: they contain a number of toxins.[48] Their dangers may be minimized or eliminated by preparatory processes such as soaking or boiling,[49] and it would seem likely, given the ubiquity and popularity of the broad bean in antiquity, that such stratagems were well known. Thus, some legumes have unpleasant, occasionally lethal side effects. Neolathyrism, for example, which may result in severe paralysis, is a possible consequence of eating vetch.[50] Ingestion of the broad bean may give rise to the medical condition known as favism (in brief, hemolytic anaemia or jaundice provoked by eating fava beans if the subject is deficient in the G6PD enzyme).[51] Favism is not a phenomenon that affects whole populations, merely those individuals lacking the enzyme (a hereditary condition). It affects some geographical areas more than others, not least Sicily and southern Italy,[52] and parts of Greece and North Africa.[53] The geographical spread is significant, and seems to indicate a split in the Graeco-Roman world.[54] The phenomenon of favism in these areas gives rise to speculation that the Pythagorean bean taboo was a tacit acknowledgement of an actual condition suffered by Pythagoras or some of his adherents.[55] The ban on consumption was a mechanism for survival by those whose life was seriously endangered by the broad bean.

The hypothesis is not unattractive. The prevalence of the enzyme deficiency amongst predominantly Greek-speaking populations may partially explain why the bean was never subject to much hostility or suspicion among Latin authors. The fact that favism has been detected in Egypt may be behind the Egyptian taboo on beans reported by Herodotus. However, the argument still does not entirely persuade. If the condition only affected certain people (and to differing degrees), how would one have been able to discern that it

(48)    Flint-Hamilton (1999), 374; Garnsey (1999), 219; Grmek (1983), 239; Parker (1983), 365. Delwiche (1978), 566.
(49)    Garnsey (1999), 220.
(50)    Flint-Hamilton (1999), 374; Garnsey (1999), 219; Grmek (1983), 239; Parker (1983), 365.
(51)    Flint-Hamilton (1999), 374.
(52)    Parker (1983), 365.
(53)    Grmek (1983), 229; 231; 240.
(54)    Grmek (1983), 231.
(55)    Grmek (1983), 239.

was the broad bean that was to blame for favistic symptoms? If many people would have been able to (and indeed did) eat broad beans on a regular basis with few ill effects, any condition arising from them would have been difficult to detect and isolate.[56] It also seems odd that if the Pythagoreans were aware of such serious symptoms, they did not refer to the dangers directly, instead choosing to shroud their warnings in allusive and allegorical language. The only observed physical effects were the bean's bloating and soporific qualities. There was no warning issued that bean consumption would perhaps result in death. It is not an explanation that is offered by later writers who would have been able to see the symptoms of favism for themselves. The obvious mystification experienced by later writers when attempting to justify the taboo makes it abundantly clear that death by broad bean was not an obvious way of explaining the taboo. Beans must have possessed a religious and cultural significance that transcended the medical facts.

If favism did exert an influence, it may have been at a subliminal level. The physiological effects of bean consumption (flatulence, bloating, disturbed sleep patterns) may have given warning of a more serious condition. Evidence for favism in antiquity may have been no more than anecdotal, or the remnants of folk wisdom, that have survived neither to us nor to the extant ancient authors. If favism manifested itself only sporadically, and only resulted in death in a small percentage of cases, it may have been viewed as a selective phenomenon, resulting from divine will.[57] If this is the case, it may provide an explanation for the manner in which they were regarded by ancient peoples, and the religious atmosphere surrounding them, although surely they cannot have been regarded with greater apprehension than plants that were genuinely and more consistently toxic to man.

Ultimately, it may be impossible to discern a coherent explanation for this form of dietary restriction. Beans' ambiguous status in Greek and Roman culture and their associations with death marked them out as an object of avoidance or as a hallowed element of religious ritual. Their principal significance seems to have been that they were a marker of Pythagorean identity, a motif immediately associated with this particular philosophical school. The vagaries of its origins elicited a number of responses in antiquity, some convincing, some less so. They all contribute to the bean's aura of mystery.

(56)   Grmek (1983), 214.
(57)   The wrath of the gods directed at those who had offended them or who had failed to perform the required propitiatory rites.

CHAPTER FOUR

# FISH

It may seem rather perverse, even misguided, to devote an entire chapter to abstention from fish. There is a remarkable enthusiasm for fish in many of our extant sources, in particular those pertaining to classical Greek societies (Athens in particular). Their writings from fifth and fourth centuries BC provide the primary source for excessive fish consumption, mainly in of the fragments preserved in the *Deipnosophistae* of Athenaeus. It is problematic to extrapolate from Athens to other Greek communities. It is likely the nature of Athenian diet (and the writings about it) was distinct from other areas of population. Many of the texts should be treated with caution: they are often fragmentary, cited in isolation, or derive from the genres of poetry or comedy. However, even if we allow for a certain amount of artistic hyperbole and distortion, or a pattern of survival of texts and archaeological evidence that presents an uncharacteristic or unrepresentative portrait of ancient dietary culture, it would still appear that fish was an abundant commodity that played a significant role, not just in gastronomy, but also in the general cultural consciousness. This is particularly evident in coastal communities. Fish and other forms of marine life were a recurrent motif that appeared not just in literary texts, but on mosaics, frescoes and coinage (on the latter, images of crabs and dolphins are prevalent).[1] Fish appeared upon the stage, in cookbooks and as the subject of philosophical dialogues. In the face of this overwhelming fondness for marine produce, any attempt to postulate individual or collective aversions would be doomed to failure.

Yet there is evidence that fish was treated as a prohibited food, through either abhorrence or reverence. While this phenomenon was never widespread,

(1)     See Jenkins (1972); Sutherland (1974). Also Wilkins and Hill (2006), 156

I believe it played a critical role in Graeco-Roman cultural self-definition. Often, contemplation of the ancient seascape and its denizens provoked a diversity of attitudes that tended to veer towards fear, distrust, even fierce hostility. Once one left the shore – *terra firma* – the watery deep became *terra incognita*. This chapter will chart the journey of fish from despised and marginalized man-eating alien to symbol of luxury and lax morals.

Some historians have sought to implement a strict division of Greek and Roman attitudes to the sea. They attempt to categorize the first as a sea-faring people, and Romans as agrarian hydrophobes.[2] This seems too crude, ignoring those who did not think themselves either Greek or Roman, and buying into rudimentary stereotypes that segments of Greek and Roman society were fond of disseminating and perpetuating. For a truly hydrophobic nation, Plutarch would have us look to the Egyptians, who thought the sea impure and alien. They were said to not even greet the sailors whom they met because they earned a living from the sea.[3]

The hostile sea is a common theme. The *Halieutica*, a poem about fishing written by Oppian in the later part of the second century AD and dedicated to the emperor Marcus Aurelius and his son Commodus, portrayed it as mysterious and inhospitable, home to monsters.[4] Even allowing for his hyperbolic language, which endeavoured to make epic the humble craft of the fisherman – an heroic canvas on which man performed daring exploits and displayed his mastery over the waves – this was plainly an environment in which man will never feel entirely at ease. It is a vast and almost unknowable province.[5]

The historian John Wilkins draws attention to the way in which both Greeks and Romans assimilated the creatures of the sea into a more familiar (and thus more controllable) sphere by the use of nomenclature.[6] Fish were named after, and frequently assigned the characteristics of, land animals, perhaps trying to absorb them into the body of human knowledge. He also

(2)     Meijer (1986), 147.
(3)     Plut *Quaest. conv.* VIII.8.729.
(4)     Opp. *Halieut*. I.40–55. In the notes to the Loeb translation of this work, A. W. Mair has the following to say on the word *kêtos*: 'denotes Whales, Dolphins, Seals, Sharks, Tunnies, and the large creatures of the sea generally'; 203, note d. His translation of it as 'Sea monsters', in line with LSJ, seems to accurately convey the sense of dread of the strange beings that inhabit the depths of the oceans. See Olson and Sens (2000), note on Archestratus frag. 35, page 40: 'The term kêtos may be used of any huge sea creature... and in biological writing is generally applied to whales (Arist. *HA* 566b2)'.
(5)     Opp. *Halieut*. I.85.
(6)     Wilkins (1993), 191.

makes the point that fish were often seen as mankind's potential nemesis. This
was not always the case. Sometimes fish were presented as being indifferent or
actively amiable (if one may use such a word in this instance) towards man.[7]
Texts presented both sides of the argument, though the general tendency was
against rather than for. On the positive side, there was reference to the pilot
fish that assisted man in locating the safety of the seashore.[8] The dolphin was
also praised because it was beloved of Poseidon.[9] The elder Pliny devoted four
chapters of his book on fish in the *Natural History* to this creature. In one
chapter he explored evidence of sympathetic relationships between man and
dolphin.[10] In the next, he explained how dolphins assisted men in catching
fish at a lake called Latera at Nemausus (Nîmes) in southern Gaul.[11]

Both Oppian and Pliny made much of the predatory nature of many sea
creatures and their threat to seafarers. It has even been claimed that it was the
octopus that provided the inspiration for the myth of the Gorgon.[12] Martial
imagery was deployed for this adversarial relationship. Pliny described an
encounter of the fleet of Alexander the Great with a shoal of tuna in terms
of a military battle.[13] Fish were not merely the enemy of mankind; given
the opportunity, they would consume his flesh. A fragment of Archestratus
preserved in Athenaeus refers to the carnivorous nature of the shark, but goes
on to state that this is not just a characteristic of this one creature, but was in
fact common to all fish.[14] A fragment of Alexis' *Women from Greece*, also in
Athenaeus, confirms this attitude:

> Living or dead, the creatures of the sea are always at war with us. If,
> for example, a ship founders, and then, as often happens, a man is
> caught while he tries to swim, they quickly gulp him down for good
> and all.[15]

(7)    It should certainly not be discounted that posited antagonistic sentiments of fish towards
       humans in texts may have been exaggerated for dramatic licence, transforming fishing
       from a rather mundane and repetitive occupation into a potential life and death struggle.
       One has only to see what the film *Jaws* did for the reputation of the great white shark.
(8)    Opp. *Halieut.* I.186–210.
(9)    Opp. *Halieut.* I.385: 'For Poseidon loves them'.
(11)   Plin. *HN* IX.9.
(12)   Elworthy (1903), 215. Elworthy rather overstates his case, believing the octopus to be
       the most fearsome and dangerous creature that lurked in ancient waters.
(13)   Plin. *HN* IX.2.3.
(14)   Frag. 35 Olson and Sens; Ath. *Deip.* 301f–2b. See Olson and Sens (2000), 40; Wilkins
       and Hill (1994), 72–73.
(15)   Kassel and Austin fr. 2.60 in Ath. *Deip.* 226 f–g; Arnott (1996), 208–210.

There are references in Homer to fish eating human flesh. In the *Iliad*, there are mentions of a slaughtered boar flung into the sea where it will be eaten by fish,[16] and how a fish will lick the blood and eat the flesh of a human corpse.[17] More generally, Homer presents a number of problems.[18] Both the *Iliad* and the *Odyssey* are noteworthy for the absence of much reference to fish as part of the heroic diet. The discrepancy between the two texts – references are slightly more frequent in the *Odyssey* – has been used to reinforce arguments that the two poems are the work of two different authors.

The epics offer a vision of diet that seems (at least in retrospect) rather curious. It is a regimen that appears to have centred on meat, roasted rather than boiled, and wine, with little or no mention of either fish or vegetables. Scouring these texts for documentary evidence of eating practices in Bronze Age Aegean cultures is unwise, but we may formulate several hypotheses to explain the omission. Possibly Homer mentioned no fish because in fact little was eaten; the texts portray existing cultural mores in place either during the period in which the events of the Trojan War were putatively set, or at the time that Homer was supposed to have lived (or perhaps both). This conjecture seems improbable for a number of reasons, not least the physiological implications of such a heavily carnivorous diet. This pattern of eating would have had catastrophic effects on the body of a warrior.[19] The poems do seem to recognize fishing as a normal activity: there is a reference in the *Odyssey* to fishing with hooks.[20] Yet, it is clear that the poet thought it something resorted to *in extremis*, with starvation imminent. Odysseus' crew chose to risk divine wrath by stealing the oxen of Helios rather than trying to catch fish (which would have been abundant and easy to procure). This surely points to rather more than mere distaste for fish (or conversely particular love of beef). Fish were either anathema to these people, or were so to the author(s). Our

(16)  Hom. *Il.* XIX.268.
(17)  Hom. *Il.* XXI.122–127.
(18)  Pl. *Resp.* III.404c; Ath. *Deip.* I 9d. Also Heath (2000), 342–352; Davidson (1996), 57–64; Davidson (1997b), 12–13; 16–17. Garnsey (1999), 73–77; Wilkins and Hill (2006), 253–260.
(19)  This may be a contentious point as, in spite of modern nutritional theories about the use of carbohydrates in athletic training, there was a tradition in Greek antiquity linking the consumption of meat with physical strength. Diogenes Laertius asserts that a certain Pythagoras (who may, or may not, have been the philosopher) was the first to alter the diet of athletes from one of figs and cheese to one of meat; *Pythag.* VIII, 12. Dalby (2003), 38. Excessive eating of beef is linked with the physical power of Hercules and Milo of Croton. See Davis (1971), 122–142 for the diet of the Roman soldier.
(20)  Hom. *Od.* XII.330–333.

difficulty is finding the motive for this aversion: disinterest, shame, reverence or something else?

Some scholars have argued the answer lay in geography: that the area of Asia Minor from which Homer was supposed to have come had a tradition of antipathy to fish.[21] This theory, claiming Smyrna as Homer's native city, suggested the 'inferiority of Phrygian fish' as the reason for their absence from Homeric diet.[22] This has found little support. It is criticized for making general what is admitted particular and parochial.[23] Others see this absence of fish as the remnants of a taboo that had become transformed into a cultural practice.[24]

Let us examine the notion of a taboo and its possible origins. Fish were taboo in Egypt and Syria and this may have exerted a powerful influence over other Mediterranean cultures. Yet, the Homeric texts fail to provide any mention of fish within a religious context. When reference is made, it is almost as an irrelevance. Perhaps the aversion to fish sprang from sentiments of dread or disgust. Plutarch saw such repulsion as perhaps springing from loathing of the sea itself.[25] He appears to link this to the attitudes of the Egyptians. In his text on the rites of Isis, he refers to the Homeric attitude to fish as being something unnecessary and superfluous.[26] He also relates the Egyptians' antipathy towards the sea.[27] The implication is that a revulsion for the sea and for the creatures it contains was a commonly held truth, of which both Homer and Egyptians were cognizant. Plutarch represents Egyptians as holding that the waters were composed of disgusting matter – that did not belong to this world. This attribution of a putrid quality to seawater is curious, but may be linked with the fact that fish do not just live in the water, but also excrete in it. They live in a quasi-faecal world, amidst a miasma of their own effluent.[28]

The aversion may have come from the notion that fish themselves were impure or polluting because they were not incorporated into the sacrificial

(21)     Scott (1917), 330.
(22)     Fraser (1923), 240.
(23)     Scott himself later came to recognize the deficiencies in this approach in a later article in the *Classical Journal* in 1936 (Vol. 32. no. 3).
(24)     Fraser (1923), 241.
(25)     Plut. *Quaest. conv.* VIII.8.729.
(26)     Plut. *De Is. et Od.,* 353D.
(27)     Plut. *De Is. et Od.,* 353E: 'In short, they [the Egyptians] believed the sea to come from pus and to lie outside the boundaries; it is neither a part nor an element but is a diseased and corrupted remnant of something else'.
(28)     A revulsion towards an animal that is supposed to exist in, or to eat, its own waste matter may be partly behind the prohibition placed by some cultures upon the flesh of pigs.

process. They were, therefore, an ineligible food. However, this may be an unproductive route to take with regard to the Homeric poems.[29] Many other foods, particularly fruit and vegetables, are similarly neglected in these texts, with no hint that they have an impure status.[30] Another proposal is that any Homeric taboo on fish may have derived from the nature of the diet of the fish themselves.[31] Fish were not appropriate for consumption by man because they were prone to consume human flesh. The stigmatization is problematic. Fish were omnivorous; they do not feed *exclusively* on human flesh.

The Pythagoreans made an explicit connection between eating the flesh of living beings and cannibalism. Through the process of *metempsychosis*, they believed that any living being could potentially house the soul of a human. However, the Pythagorean biographical texts were confused over the status of fish within diet. Fish were perceived as occupying a position that was analogous to, but separate and distinct from meat, since not all fish were regarded as forbidden.[32] Avoidance of meat was a necessary precaution against inadvertent cannibalism but the attitude to fish was ambivalent. Again, a factor that may have counted against fish was their taste for humans: by attempting to eat people they were possibly regarded as subverting a natural hierarchy.

Fish were not the only scavengers in Homer. Birds, dogs and fish are all associated with dead bodies and it may be significant that fish and birds are only eaten in extreme circumstances, and dogs not at all.[33] But the likelihood that it was solely their appetites that made them taboo is small. Birds do not feed exclusively (or mostly at all) on human flesh, and dogs, when domesticated, are taught (or constrained) not to eat it. A taboo or disinclination might have existed in Homeric times for simpler reasons: birds and fish exist at a distance from the realm of man, they were truly alien beasts.

The case for dogs is quite opposite. Their domestication, and their use in shepherding and hunting, as well as for protection,[34] rendered them perhaps

---

(29)   Wilkins notes that the Homeric poets were not averse to the sea, citing the inventory of regal properties in *Od.* XIX.109–114; Wilkins and Hill (2006), 256. Also Ath. *Deip.* 9d for Homeric references to fish as a source of wealth and symbol of abundance.

(30)   However, maybe the existence of fish, vegetables and fruit is implied by the use of the vague term *eidata polla* (a multitude of foodstuffs), Hom. *Od.* XVII.95. See Wilkins and Hill (2006), 257.

(31)   Combellack (1953).

(32)   Iambl. *VP* 109 specifies the *melanouros* and *erythrinus*. Diog. Laert. *Pythag.* VIII. 19 also lists the former, but does not mention the *erythrinus*, but instead the red mullet.

(33)   Combellack (1953), 260.

(34)   Hes. *Op.* 603–605.

too close to man for comfort. Yet there were instances of their being killed and even eaten. Plutarch mentions that puppies were commonly sacrificed to the goddess Hecate, and dogs were sacrificed during the Roman festival of Lupercalia.[35] Galen noted that at least some communities were happy to consume the flesh of dogs. The historian of Greek religion, Robert Parker, highlights the sometimes degraded status of the dog, noting its exclusion from sacred sites such as Delos, and its lowly place in the hierarchy of sacrificial animals.[36] This appears to confirm the notion of the dog as scavenger, but nevertheless one may make a case for some feeling of sympathy between dog and man. We know that Greeks kept dogs as pets.[37] There are in existence records of approximately four hundred dog names from antiquity.[38]

A sympathetic and symbiotic rapport between man and beast was offered as reason for the hallowed status of the dolphin; its intelligence and apparently congenial nature raised it above the mass of other aquatic creatures. Wilkins notes the sacred standing of the dolphin within Graeco-Roman culture, but also observes that in some other civilizations, it was rather less valued.[39] The Mossynoeci (people who lived on the southern shores of the Black Sea, west of Trebizond) used dolphin fat in their cuisine, as well as pickling and storing slices of dolphin flesh.[40] Clearly, the dolphin's status was not absolute. This is not to say that the dolphin was the only form of marine life capable of arousing feelings of tenderness. Porphyry relates the implausible tale of the Roman triumvir Crassus (who ruled with Pompey and Julius Caesar) and his pet lamprey. This fish would answer when its name was called, and its death elicited from its master considerably more grief than that of his three children.[41]

Another plausible hypothesis for the exclusion of fish from Homer is that the author(s) chose to describe the warriors' diet in these terms and that fish

(35)     Plut.*Quaest. Rom.* LII; LXVII. Lupercalia (on the ides of February) celebrated Lupercus, the god of shepherds, as well as Lupa, the she-wolf who suckled Romulus and Remus. At the festival, two goats and a dog were sacrificed and thongs were made from the skins of the offerings. Adepts then ran a predetermined route round the city lashing young girls and women who gathered along the way: a stroke of the lash would ensure fertility and banish sterility.

(36)     Parker (1983), 357–358.

(37)     Lonsdale (1979), 150.

(38)     Lonsdale (1979), 149.

(39)     Wilkins and Hill (2006), 155.

(40)     Xen. *An.* V.4.28; Wilkins and Hill (2006), 155.

(41)     Porph. *Abst.* 3.5. See Clark (2000), 166 note 403, which notes that Plutarch mentions this in *De soll. an.* 976f but omits the three children. See Ward (1974), 185–186 for argument that the Crassus mentioned is not the *triumvir*, but the orator Lucius Crassus.

was considered food unfit for heroes.[42] Plato made reference to this dietary idiosyncrasy in the *Republic*.[43] For him, Achilles and the rest were akin to demigods, and their diet reflected this: like the immortals, they consumed animal flesh (although, obviously, they did not consume the same parts of the carcass that sacrificial ritual assigned to the gods). The gods rejected the flesh of fish, and so did the Homeric warriors. The critic Peter Garnsey posits that the author of the *Iliad* and the *Odyssey,* as they were interpreted in the *Deipnosophistae* of Athenaeus, was endeavouring to map onto his literary landscape a dietary ideal. This had a didactic function: it sought to influence peer behaviour.[44]

Within the context of later societies (in particular, that of classical Athens), fish came to be regarded as a mark of ostentatious wealth and luxurious living, enjoyed by the gluttonous, the effeminate and the corrupt. If Plato were thus reflecting reality as he knew it, fish would have been an entirely inappropriate foodstuff for an Achilles or an Odysseus. Plutarch made a similar point about Homeric simplicity.[45] In this strain of thought, fish was equated not with urbanity and sophistication, but with dissolute effeminacy. The warriors before Troy represented the pure and uncorrupted heroic archetype.

So far, I have concentrated largely upon Greek attitudes. Superficially, the beliefs and anxieties of the Romans appear to mirror them, proceeding from an initial distrust or distaste for fish as something unfamiliar and alien to an enthusiastic embrace of all things piscine. This latter-day conversion to seafood was, as the Greeks, allied to a nervousness about its ideological implications, particularly from those who linked eating fish with autocracy on the one hand and wanton behaviour on the other, hence a betrayal of cultural roots. The texts of the imperial period offer an amalgam of the poetic, the satirical and the scientific. Oppian transported the profession of the fisherman into the realms of the epic; the elder Pliny and Galen proposed an alternative view, largely shorn of religious or folkloric embellishment.

Just as Plato identified the eating of fish with profligacy and weakness, an aberration from the austere diet of an earlier epoch, so frequently Latin writers saw fish as representing simultaneously development and degeneration. A

---

(42)     There is one another possibility, albeit hugely implausible: that all references to fish were excised from the material during some later period. However, it would be difficult to discern a motive for such action.

(43)     Pl. *Resp.* III.404bc. See also Heath (2000),342–352.

(44)     Garnsey (1999), 76.

(45)     Plut. *Quaest. conv.* IV.4.668F.

transformation of diet formed part of the process whereby a society became more sophisticated and complex, but this was not always assumed to be a good thing. Social and cultural mutation could mean a shift away from idealized origins. In Book VI of *Fasti*, Ovid referred to a period when diet was simpler and, pointedly, fish were not eaten.

> You ask why we eat greasy bacon-fat on the Kalends,
> And why we mix beans with parched grain?
> She is an ancient goddess, nourished by familiar food,
> No epicure to seek out alien dainties.
> In ancient times the fish still swam unharmed,
> And the oysters were safe in their shells.[46]

The elder Pliny, too, warned against eating seafood:

> But why do I mention these trifles when moral corruption and luxury spring from another source in greater abundance than from the genus shellfish?[47]

In short, fish was perceived as being both a symptom of, and an agent for increasing and promoting luxurious behaviour.

Even if fish were a prized commodity, the status of fishermen was less exalted. There was a definite schism between purchasing and consuming the fish and the physical act of catching it.[48] The ancient seascape could be seen as a bleak realm in which man does not belong, and sea-fishermen could possess a marginal status.[49] Even those who greatly cherished fish felt the need to distance themselves from the demeaning activity of catching it. Plutarch thought it more correct to purchase fish than to catch them.[50]

In Greece and Rome, certain fish were able to command enormous sums of money, the larger species especially.[51] Such trafficking might suffer from the

---

(46)     Ov. *Fast*. VI.169–182. Translation A.S. Kline, http://www.poetryintranslation.com/klineasfasti.htm.

(47)     Plin. *HN* IX.liii.34. See also Wilkins (2000), Ch. 6 'Luxurious Eating in Comedy', 257–311.

(48)     If we are to believe Athenian comedy, the mediator between these worlds, that of the artisan and the consumer – the fish seller – was also a troublesome and untrustworthy figure.

(49)     Purcell (1995), 135.

(50)     Plut. *De soll. an.* 965e–966b.

(51)     Davidson (1995), 135.

FISH

63

taint of 'élitism', something perhaps disliked or mistrusted in a community
wary of autocratic forms of government, but even so, there were plenty of
people who seemed to value fish over meat, even when the latter was available.
Aelian's report of this situation pertaining on Rhodes may be no more than
a reflection of its (literal) insularity,[52] but with the development of fish farms
during the late Roman republic and early imperial period, fish and seafood
became not merely esteemed, prized for taste, but valued possessions in
themselves. They were frequently not even eaten, but lived as symbols of
affluence, privilege and refinement. Varro recounts the enormous sums spent
on pisciculture. Gaius Lucius Hirrus was said to have earned twelve thousand
sesterces from the buildings around his fishponds, and this income was all
spent on food for the fish.[53]

   To balance this picture, fish could occupy a position at the very opposite
end of the social and economic spectrum. Small fish could be caught by individuals, either from the shore or from small boats. These largely bypassed
the market economy, being consumed by the fishermen themselves, or sold/
bartered within the family or their immediate circle. These were not the
enormous creatures worthy of a powerful ruler, a Polycrates or a Domitian,[54]
but they were easy to obtain. Catches did not depend on having the where-
withal to own or equip a boat, nor on the vagaries of weather. Another
factor which ensured that fish were available to all sectors of society was the
widespread adoption of salting and preservation and the production of fish
sauce (*garum* or *liquamen*).[55] Preservation also allowed access to fish products
at any season of the year.

   Our discussion has concentrated on sea fishing, for here the most significant matters of cultural identity were forged. But people also ate river fish,
though the catch usually commanded a lower price. Some of the arguments
advanced for and against eating fish would have been applicable to both sorts.
Galen was not a fan of freshwater fish, unless from fast-flowing streams and
rivers. Swamps, marshes and other stagnant waters were not good.[56] Slow or
sluggish flows ran the risk of sewage pollution,[57] and catches from polluted
waters were less expensive still. Galen talks of an eel that lived in the Tiber

(52)    Ael. *VH.* I.28.
(53)    Varro *Rust.* II.xvii.2–9.
(54)    Hdt. III.42; Juv. IV. Wilkins (1993); Purcell (1995).
(55)    Curtis (2001), 402–417.
(56)    Gal. *De al. fac.* 6.709–738 K.
(57)    Gal. *De al. fac.* 6.722–723 K.

which was cheap in Rome because the sewage made it taste unpleasant.[58] The penurious would have had to balance the low price against the disagreeable taste and the very real hazard of falling ill. Varro, too, speaks disparagingly of freshwater fish, fit only for the poor.[59]

It will come as no surprise to discover that the main proponents of a meat-free diet – the Pythagoreans, Plutarch, Porphyry – also advocated turning away from food from the waters.[60] But there was one significant difference between meat and fish in an ancient context. Meat bore certain connotations as part of ritual sacrifice. Fish presented less of a problem in this respect.[61] This rendered it, in some ways, an inherently selfish foodstuff in that it was not shared with any of the gods. However, there were some sacred fish. Diogenes Laertius, in his life of Pythagoras, mentions the red mullet and the *melanouros*, although he does not give a reason for their sanctified status.[62] Iamblichus also makes reference to the blacktail and the erythrinos fish, and maintained the Pythagoreans thought they belonged to the infernal deities.[63] This would explain the Pythagorean prohibition on the eating of certain 'sacred' fish as Diogenes Laertius asserted that they believed that it was inappropriate for mortals and immortals to partake of the same food.[64] Sacred fish, it seems, also fell into the category of belonging to the gods, although not subject to sacrificial slaughter.

There is plenty of evidence that fish were entities that could be feared or revered, especially if they seemed to be sympathetic or helpful to man, or connected in some way with a specific deity.[65] However, it seems not to have been a characteristic of Graeco-Roman peoples to abstain from fish for religious reasons, even if they were cited as one of the categories forbidden

(58)    Gal. *De al. fac.* 6.722 K.
(59)    Varro *Rust.* II.xvii.2–9.
(60)    Iamb. *VP* 98 asserts that not all fish were taboo for the Pythagoreans. Laertius also denies a blanket piscine proscription. According to him, only the red mullet and *melanouros* were taboo; Diog. Laert. *Pythag.* VIII.19
(61)    Fish were not generally sacrificed, although there were exceptions; Ath. *Deip.* 297c for the sacrifice of conger eels by the Boeotians, and tuna in Attica.
(62)    Diog. Laert. *Pythag.* VIII.19. However, later, he refers to abstention from meat and fish (specifically mullets) in the context of purification (VIII.33). However, it is not entirely clear whether the exhortation was meant to apply to all species of fish.
(63)    Iamb. *VP* 24.109.
(64)    Diog. Laert. *Pythag.* VIII.34.
(65)    For example, Paus. XLI.4–8. Pausanias describes a sanctuary to Eurymone in Phigalia, Arcadia. It was believed that she was a daughter of Ocean. Although Pausanias did not see the image of Eurymone himself, he was informed that the wooden image therein represented a figure that was half-human and half-fish.

to the initiates of the Eleusinian mysteries, along with domestic fowl, beans, apples and pomegranates.[66] Robert Parker notes similar rules in connection to the Haloa, an Eleusinian festival devoted to Demeter and fertility.[67] Fish abstention was generally regarded by Greeks as something that alien cultures did, in particular the Egyptians and the Syrians. Egyptian priests had precepts that prohibited them from eating fish, although this did not extend to the whole population.[68] Fish abstention amongst the population was frequently selective: the people of Oxyrynchus did not consume those fish that were caught with a hook, believing them to be impure, whilst those who lived at Syene did not eat the sea bream, believing it to be a herald of the rising of the Nile. Herodotus maintained that only two sorts of fish were held in sanctity by the Egyptians – the lepidotus and the eel. These were regarded as sacred to the Nile.[69]

There are many references to the worship of the Syrian goddess known variously as Derceto, Astarte and Atargatis.[70] Diodorus Siculus said that Derceto was turned into a fish through the wrath of Aphrodite, and this was why Syrians did not eat fish, instead revered them.[71] In Athenaeus, it is asserted that, according to the Stoic Antipater of Tarsus, the edict prohibiting fish consumption derives from a desire to prevent anyone 'except Gatis' (Gatis being the queen of Syria) eating fish.[72] A similar explanation is offered by Mnaseas, in *On Asia*.[73] He relates that they were the preferred tribute of a cruel ruler, Queen Atargatis (note the difference in name). Lucian's *De Dea Syria* deals extensively with the rites of this cult of Atargatis. He refers to a half-human, half-fish effigy, representing Derceto, in Phoenicia. However, he says that the image at the temple at Hierapolis is all woman. There is mention of the fish taboo, and he refers to a lake near the temple where fish were raised.[74] Severe punishments were threatened to those who did not properly revere and care for the sacred fish:

(66)     Porph. *Abst.* 4.16. See Clark (2000), page 189, note 642.
(67)     Parker (1983), 358.
(68)     Hooke (1961), 535; Plut. *De Is. et Os.*353C–D.
(69)     Hdt. II.72.
(70)     See Burkert (1983), 204–207; Gilhus (2006), 93.
(71)     Diod. Sic. II.4.2–4.
(72)     Ath. *Deip.* 346d.
(73)     F.H.G.iii.155; Ath. *Deip.* 346d–e..
(74)     Lucian *Syr. D.* 45. There is also a reference in Xenophon to sacred fish, revered by the Syrians in the Chalus river; Xen. *An.*1.4.9.

The superstitious believe of the Syrian goddess that if someone were
to eat small fish or sardines, she will eat through his shins, burn his
body with ulcers and melt his liver. [75]

The punishment is aimed not just at those who consume the larger and more
prestigious species of fish, but any marine life. This rather florid description of
the potential fate of fish abusers is reinforced by an inscription from Smyrna
which threatens the destruction of those who insult fish or attempt to steal
them.[76] A taboo on fish was also associated with rites connected with the
worship of Cybele.[77]

It seems evident that fish veneration, while not entirely absent from Greece
and Rome, was more conspicuous in the ideological systems of neighbouring
cultures. A more significant influence on Greek and Roman attitudes may have
been the way fish was placed within the diet. If one looks at the way classical
Greek thought broke down its idealized dietary regimen into a threefold
division of *opson*, *sitos*, and *oinos* (put crudely, meat/fish/vegetables, cereal
and wine), the first element was deemed to occupy a subordinate role.[78] Both
Plato and Xenophon used the form of the Socratic dialogue to examine the
formulation of this dietary division.[79] It is not that *opson* is inherently bad.
Indeed, it is a necessary part of the diet. However, it must not be allowed
to take a predominant position, lest the components of the diet become
unbalanced.

These many strands of fishy ideologies are confusing and ambiguous.
They point to an apparent *volte-face* in Greek and Roman cultures. Fish are
transformed from something that was despised and marginal in the Homeric
texts, to a commodity that was coveted and revered, yet was feared for its
power to corrupt. It may not be unreasonable to suggest that this shift may

(75)    Plut. *De superst.* 170D.
(76)    Syll.³ 997.
(77)    Scott (1922), 226.
(78)    LSJ notes that *opson* was generally thought of as signifying meat, but at Athens
        was mostly understood as meaning fish. It also has the meaning of 'anything eaten
        with bread', or 'seasoning', or 'sauce'. It may be helpful to us to view the *opson*/*sitos*
        division in terms of a protein/carbohydrate split. See Davidson (1995), 205–207.
        Davidson appreciates the difficulty of determining a precise definition of *opson*, and
        locating it within this dietary system: 'It is a necessary element of the diet and yet
        somehow superfluous to it'. I am not sure that Davidson is correct in defining it as
        a superfluous element; even Plato in *Resp.* allowed fruit and vegetables into the diet.
(79)    Xen. *Mem.*3.14; Pl. *Resp.* 2.372a–373c.

have accompanied growing cultural, political and economic confidence, a self-assurance marked by maritime expansion. The frequent references to compulsive fish eating in Athenian comedies came when Athenian imperial ambitions ensured a steady flow of tribute into the city from its overseas possessions. Was the incidence of fish gluttony in the fourth century, when tribute to Athens had dried up, a display of some form of nostalgia? Similarly, the Roman mania for fish farms developed as the state's tendrils spread over the Mediterranean. There was a growing sense of control, even mastery, over the waves. Travel became safer as the threat of pirates was removed.[80] Fish fall under human domination as the sea is brought under control. Both Athens and Rome experienced the influx of wealth that accompanied both political dominion and increased trading opportunities. Fish become almost synonymous with material wealth and political potency. The contents of a Roman fish farm were not there to be eaten, but to be admired. They were a valuable piece of property that signified wealth and social status; just as the purchase of a large fish in the Athenian agora showed the affluence of the consumer (although a rich man eating cheap fish may be taken for an arrant miser).

This equating of fish and affluence carries intriguing ideological implications.[81] The consumption of fish was a signifier of urban sophistication, and was an inherently secular and *human* activity. It was a selfish foodstuff, not offering any part of itself to the gods, nor was it divided among the diners. It was consumed not for its ritual significance but for the sake of gastronomic gratification. In a sense, it is hardly surprising that it should have been the signal for social anxiety. The transition from utilitarian to hedonistic was a sign of societies in the process of mutation. Increased wealth meant greater freedom from the shackles of self-sustenance and more time that could be devoted to pleasure. Anxieties that connect increased affluence across the social spectrum with the disintegration of morality are themes that concern social commentators even in modern Western societies. Inevitably, the social spectrum is limited almost exclusively to the élite. It is the affluent who suffer paroxysms of cultural angst.

Scholars are far from unanimous about the importance of fish in ancient Mediterranean diet. Sallares and Gallant warn about the perils of using literary texts to form hypotheses about historical processes. Given that so much of our

(80)    App. *Rom. Hist.* XII.xiv.94–96 for Pompey's crushing of piracy in the Mediterranean in 67 BC.
(81)    Davidson (1997b), 20.

information about a mania for fish within Greek culture comes from Athenian comedies, there is a risk that we may fall prey to treating the hyperbole of the stage as documentary evidence and view Athens as the same as other Greek communities.[82] This is also a concern when we look at cities such as Rome, Alexandria or Ephesus. One cannot extrapolate from them a homogeneity of diet across swathes of territories. These urban maelstroms of disparate cultures and religions cannot be convincingly compared to small village communities located in provincial backwaters.

Gallant in particular feels that the importance of fish in classical Greek diet has been greatly exaggerated. In his *Fisherman's Tale*, he describes how ancient fishing techniques were small-scale and labour-intensive. They were subject to the vagaries of migration (not always accurately predictable). Hence, he sees fish as marginal.[83] It is a perplexing state of affairs. Gallant's thesis is plausible, particularly his assertion that the movement of fish (particularly the pelagic species such as mackerel and tuna) was too unpredictable to permit it the status of dietary or economic staple. Yet the extant literature from both Greek and Roman sources affords fish huge ideological weight. If we accept Gallant's theory, then we are compelled to interpret literary representations of fishing and fish (whether large or small) as something more than tracts about food and diet. Fish become ideological constructs of identity; they are status markers. They become a metaphor that revolves around notions of aspiration or derogation. Once, caviar and champagne were regarded as useful signifiers in the Western world. These words would instantly conjure up images of wealth and sophistication. It may be profitable to think of fish in Graeco-Roman antiquity in a similar way. It was a useful linguistic and conceptual tool which enabled a writer to use the word fish as an ultra-dense mass of imagery and innuendo, understood within the confines of that culture as representing something more subtle and complex. Fish had taken on a role that went far beyond its actuality. The extent to which it actually featured in the diet may be not as important as first thought.

All the evidence so far has suggested a widespread anxiety in Graeco-Roman about the sea and the forms of life that it contained. Yet, if we accept this analysis, this was not the prime focus of their fear. Rather, it was an apprehension about the way wealth and foreign cultural influences were transforming indigenous societies. This oozes from the ancient texts and reflects

(82)    Gallant (1985), 12.
(83)    Gallant (1985), 42.

the concerns of the well-heeled. Wealth becomes spread throughout the social order, invariably facilitating a greater degree of social mobility. Eating fish could be a revolutionary act.[84]

Actual habitual abstention from fish within these cultures was rare. The Pythagoreans and others who espoused a vegetarian diet were in a definite minority. Fish exerted alternating forces of repulsion and attraction, but in general people seem not to have desisted from fish consumption (even with all those dubious moral connotations). The concern with fish seems to have been ideological. It appears that abstention from fish was viewed as something foreigners did. Unusual attitudes to fish could be a method of culturally defining other races. Herodotus notes that there were three Babylonian tribes that ate nothing but fish.[85] Of course, such a diet seems highly unlikely, and may just have been an example of the Herodotean 'mirror', by which the 'normality' of Greek customs were defined as the inverse of other alien practices.[86] If these Babylonians are defined as eating only fish, surely it is to contrast them with Greeks who have a 'proper' balanced diet, or who eat rather more meat than fish (and more cereal than meat). A repudiation of fish may have been as abnormal in the same way as a diet that was comprised exclusively of fish.

An absolute proscription was regarded as the hallmark of other races, something unnatural: their diets were unbalanced. This may have been one of the fears that lay behind the criticism of *opsophagia* (the excessive desire to eat only *opson* – fish and meat): it could have been construed as the start of an inexorable slide towards the behaviour of the other. It undermined cultural identity. This is difficult to reconcile with the deficiency of fish in the Homeric diet. Lack of fish in Homer is equated with purity and heroic virtue, not with primitivism. Ultimately, it is difficult to say why a dearth of fish in Homer was lauded, while fish abstention in other cultures was viewed with mistrust. Perhaps it was simply nostalgia for simpler times, a rose-tinted view of the past inspired by the tumult and turbulence of social and economic change. It is surely this that concerns writers such as Athenaeus and Plutarch; the search for identity in a constructed purer past amidst the uncertainty of (their) modernity. The upsurge in fish-eating and the veneration of fish as a supremely

(84)    Davidson (1993) for fish as a destabilizing influence in classical Athenian society.
(85)    Hdt. I.200. Also, II.92 for Egyptian marsh dwellers who also subsisted only on fish, in this instance dried.
(86)    Hartog (1988). See Davidson (1997b), 309–315.

desirable foodstuff occurred during periods when territorial expansion in the Greek and Roman world brought a substantial influx of wealth and immigrants, accentuating and accelerating the process of hybridization.

One cannot fail to notice the repeated connection made in antiquity between the consumption of fish and social status. Small fish are consumed by those at the lower end of the social spectrum; the larger species were reserved for the moneyed and the politically dominant. Embedded within this analysis is the ideological dichotomy that both positions may be simultaneously good and bad. Poverty is to be despised but may in some way be eulogized as being closer to an untainted and uncorrupted archetype. Luxury may signify progress, but with it brings the potential to erode the qualities that made that success achievable. If fish were in any way marginal to ancient diet, its ideological significance was such that it burned itself onto the ancient Mediterranean consciousness.

CHAPTER FIVE

# THE DIETARY LAWS OF THE JEWS

In the Graeco-Roman world, one race seems to have been most associated with dietary restriction (at least in the popular imagination): the Jews. Their dietary discipline was enshrined in in the pages of their sacred writings and was just one component of a rigorous table of behavioural laws that the pious were required to obey. These regulations were scrupulously delineated so that they were as unambiguous as possible, ensuring that misunderstandings were eliminated and could not prove a hindrance to a correct adherence.

I shall concentrate upon some of the cultural practices of the Jews as they manifested themselves in the Diaspora communities outside, rather than within Judea. My reasons are twofold. Firstly, the existence of a geographically scattered community, united by a set of directives for living, enables us to test the effectiveness of these regulations.[1] Jewish religious laws were exacting and arduous, especially when individuals and groups were far from their (spiritual) homeland and the focussing influence of the Temple. Adherence was easier in communities that were largely or exclusively Jewish than where Jews were the minority. Secondly, since the purpose of the dietary laws was both social cohesion and to trace a bold demarcation between Jew and Gentile, it is principally in the context of the Diaspora that one may see this in operation. The cultural and ethnic friction between Jews and other groups enables an analysis of issues of dietary restriction and its impact upon identity.

I have largely ignored their practice of ritual fasting. This is not to deny that these occasional periods of complete abstention were significant. They fasted

(1)     See Williams (2000), 306: '...Diasporan Jewry is of far greater relevance to the issues of culture, identity and power in the Roman empire [than the Jews of Judea]'.

for various reasons: for atonement, as a mark of grief or for the purgation of sin.[2] However, it was not a quotidian element of Judaism, and seems to have been practised only in exceptional circumstances.[3] It was an affirmative, not a nihilistic act, and its aim was not death but the achievement of a direct divine intervention. It was a temporary, not an absolute practice. It was not an attempt to subdue bodily functions, nor even to mortify and eradicate the flesh. This impulse towards chastity, virginity and the annihilation of sexual urges was a characteristic of later Christian dietary asceticism, not of Judaism. If the concern of this investigation is to establish causal links between the perception and formation of identity and the imposition of food restrictions, it would seem fruitful to focus upon recurring elements of behaviour, rather than lending disproportionate significance to extraordinary acts of self-denial.

Another reason for passing over the subject is that the Graeco-Roman majority was itself familiar with religious fasting.[4] One of the most notable Greek fasts was the second day of the Athenian Thesmophoria, known as the *Nesteia*. Our best evidence for this is Aristophanes' *Thesmophoriazusae*.[5] There is also a passing reference in the *Birds*.[6] Plutarch, in his essay on Isis and Osiris, posits this fast imitates Egyptian rites.[7] It lasted for but one day. Longer periods of abstinence were a feature neither of Judaism nor of Greek or Roman religion. Hence it is improbable that fasting was a badge of cultural identity or of ethnic demarcation that would antagonize mainstream thought in the Graeco-Roman world.

Jewish exceptionalism (at least as recognized by Greek and Latin commentators) consisted in a belief in a single god, the aniconic nature of their worship of this deity, the practice of male circumcision, the observance of the Sabbath as a day of rest, and submission to strict dietary legislation. To these may be added occasional periods of fasting and ritual ablutions. These defined the Jewish experience, even if in the eyes of external observers some of them appeared of greater significance (or at least more noticeable) than others.

(2)    Grimm (1996), 20–24; also Grimm (1995), 225–40.

(3)    The actual number of fast days in the Jewish calendar are relatively few, commemorating catastrophic or exceptional events in the history of the Jewish people, including the obliteration of the Temples, the fall of Jerusalem, and *Yom Kippur*, the Day of Atonement; Sigal (1988), 250; Jacobs (1995), 164.

(4)    Dillon (2002), 113.

(5)    Ar. *Thesm.* 949; 984. See Detienne (1977), 99–122; Burkert (1985), 242–246; Wilkins and Hill (2006), 97–98.

(6)    Ar. *Av.* 1519.

(7)    Plut. *De Is. et Os.* 378E. See also Harrison (1922), 129.

In reporting Jewish dietary laws, Gentile commentators largely ignored the details and focused on their refusal to eat pork. The complex set of rules defining the type and species of animals that were permissible to Jews and the stringent legislation that governed the process of slaughter were barely noticed. These laws were set down in the Old Testament books of Deuteronomy and Leviticus.[8] They were divided into prohibitions and allowances pertaining to creatures of the land, those of the sea and those of the air. Of the first category, those judged acceptable were those animals that possessed cloven hooves and chewed the cud.[9] Animals had to fulfil both prerequisites; one or other was held to be insufficient. In Deuteronomy are listed the animals it was permitted to consume. These included the ox, the sheep, the goat and the antelope.[10] Species which failed the test (because they possessed but one of the necessary qualifications) included the camel, the hare, the badger and the pig.[11] They were forbidden because they are deemed 'unclean' or impure.[12] The rules expressly forbid not just the ingestion of the flesh but any physical contact with the cadaver. Pollution may be spread by touch as well as by taste. A similar concern with the hazard of contamination is shared by commentators on the Pythagorean bean taboo.

Of aquatic creatures, only fish that possessed scales and fins were allowed. There was also a lengthy list of forbidden birds. The inventory's guiding rationale seems to have been the elimination from the diet of flesh-eating birds, such as the eagle, the vulture and the kite.[13] Winged insects were also illicit, apart from a few such as the locust and the grasshopper.[14] Also forbidden were animals that had died of natural causes, and a rather strange embargo against boiling a kid in its mother's milk, usually understood to indicate that meat and dairy products were not to be mixed, neither in preparation nor in consumption.[15] It was stressed that impurity may arise if any clothes or cooking utensils came into contact with prohibited substances.[16] Beyond the continued emphasis that restricted foods are unclean and carry the stain of pollution, no explanation is provided as to why this dietary legislation should

(8)     *Deut.* 14; *Levit.* 11.
(9)     *Deut.* 14, 6; *Levit.* 11, 3.
(10)    *Deut.* 14, 4–5.
(11)    *Deut.* 14, 7–8; *Levit.* 11, 4–8.
(12)    *Levit.* 11, 8.
(13)    *Levit.* 11, 13–19; *Deut.* 14, 11–18.
(14)    *Levit.* 11, 20–23; *Deut* 14, 19–20.
(15)    *Deut.* 14, 21. However, Deuteronomy states that it is acceptable to give it to a stranger or sell it to alien peoples.

be obeyed. The fact that they are directives from God may have been sufficient justification, with no further reasons required. Nonetheless, in other, later texts, there was some attempt to suggest reasons behind these divine orders.

An author who acted as a bridge between Hellenistic philosophy and Jewish beliefs was Philo of Alexandria, sometimes called Philo Judaeus (20 BC–AD 50). He has much to say on the question of diet. He maintained that the creatures whose flesh was forbidden in the sacred texts were, in fact, the tastiest and the fattest. Their prohibition was designed to prevent temptation towards the sin of gluttony, which threatened to imperil both soul and body.[17] The most delectable creature of the land was the pig, and fish that lacked scales were the tastiest denizens of the deep. These would have included the dolphin, the porpoise and various species of whale. The dietary laws were established to ensure Jewish people led an abstemious and virtuous life.[18] Philo believed that Moses intended the legislation to achieve a mean that lay somewhere between extreme frugality and sheer luxuriousness.[19]

Let us consider Philo's explanation for its genesis. Foods were forbidden because of their tendency to luxury and gluttony, venal sins. The proscription of the finest flesh was intended to promote frugality and a degree of asceticism. An impulse towards abstemiousness, and the causal linking of gluttony with vice (be it effeminacy, moral laxity or corruption) was not a solely Jewish phenomenon. It was offered as one explanation for the food restrictions of Pythagoreans,[20] as it was for the apparent simplicity of the diet of the heroes of the *Iliad* and the *Odyssey*.[21] Given its similarity to other strains of ascetic philosophical thought in Graeco-Roman culture, it is tempting to view Philo's explanation as likely to appeal to the sensibilities of a literate and learned non-Jewish readership.

Perhaps Philo was unsure that logic was a sufficient explanation for he develops his interpretation along wildly metaphorical and symbolic lines. He notes that Deuteronomy lists ten categories of acceptable animals: ten, of course, is a perfect and sacred number. Philo credits Moses with rigorous

(16)    *Levit.* 11, 24-40.
(17)    Philo *The Special Laws* IV, 100.
(18)    Cf Ath. *Deip.* 9d.
(19)    Philo *The Special Laws* IV, 102. The two extremes of behaviour are represented by, on one hand, the Spartans and, on the other, the Ionians and the Sybarites.
(20)    Diog. Laert. *Pythag.* VIII.13.
(21)    Pl. *Resp.* III.404bc; Plut. *Quaest. conv.* IV 4.668F. Ath. *Deip.* 9d. Philo looks at Moses in a similar way to the way Diogenes Laertius treats Pythagoras and Athenaeus looks at Homer; as a paragon of archaic virtue and as a model for virtuous living.

mathematical and numeric logic.[22] He then reiterates biblical criteria for dietary purity and tries to justify them in terms of spiritual and moral pollution.[23] Thus the cloven hoof represents the double aspect of life, one of vice, the other of virtue. An uncloven hoof would mean that somehow good and evil spring from the same source.[24] Chewing the cud also gets its symbolic interpretation: digestion is an allegory of the transmission of knowledge from teacher to pupil and its comprehension and retention.[25]

These improbable rationalizations continue. Scaleless fish represent souls devoted to luxury and pleasure, while those with scales and fins are linked to self-restraint.[26] Prohibited reptiles epitomize the sins of passion and gluttony.[27] Outlawed birds were either raptors or feasted on carrion.[28] In closing, he talks of the embargo upon the carcasses of animals that have died of natural causes, or have been killed by other animals, and the ban upon consumption of blood and fat (blood because it is the essence of life, and fat because it was the richest part of the animal and thus associated with superfluity and extravagance).[29]

The division of foods into clean and unclean relies on concepts of spiritual corruption and physical contamination. This exegesis seems to shy away from the sanction of divine authority, although the biblical texts are explicit that these are divine commands. It does not seem likely that Philo thought his Gentile readership would balk at the notion of the sanctity of divine authority (surely a readily comprehensible concept to both poly- and mono-theists). However, Philo does not say that the commandments are without reason, nor that they should be obeyed absolutely, without question. They are presented, rather, as the Mosaic attempt to achieve temperance. This found parallels beyond Judea. Pythagorean taboos and exclusions were explained in very similar fashion. Some saw an explicit relationship between the two, with Pythagoras adopting many tenets of Jewish law.[30]

The points of contact between Judaism and broader Mediterranean taboos or exclusions were many and various. Animals might be hallowed as

(22) Philo *The Special Laws* IV, 105.
(23) Philo *The Special Laws* IV, 106.
(24) Philo *The Special Laws* IV, 108–109.
(25) Philo *The Special Laws* IV, 108–109.
(26) Philo *The Special Laws* IV, 110–112. This is similar to the hierarchy of animals in the *Timaeus*. Pl. *Ti.* 91d–92b; Gilhus (2006), 86.
(27) Philo *The Special Laws* IV, 113–115.
(28) Philo *The Special Laws* IV, 116–118.
(29) Philo *The Special Laws* IV, 119–125.
(30) Hermippus of Smyrna *De Pythagora* apud: Joseph. *Ap.* I, 165.

either earthly manifestations of the divine (as in the case of the attitude of the Egyptians towards animals) or under divine guardianship (the Syrian ban on the eating of fish, associated with the worship of the goddess Atargatis or, for example, the Latin taboo on the woodpecker, possibly sacred to Mars).[31] The notion of foods as pure or impure was current beyond Israel, though perhaps the idea that a foodstuff could be taboo for a limited period, as the result of its connections with particular religious rituals, was its more normal expression. The absolute character of the Jewish regulations and their rigidity may have been somewhat alien, but, in general, they should have provoked little surprise or comment from external commentators. The fact that they did lies in one particular element – the abstention from the flesh of swine.

The social anthropologist Mary Douglas has made an analysis of Jewish dietary rules.[32] She notes that scholarly interpretation has typically regarded them as absolute instructions to enforce discipline or as metaphors for sin and virtue.[33] She dismisses these arguments, as well as the view that advocates a wholly separatist sentiment on behalf of the Jews; a quest to eradicate completely exotic and extraneous influences that could possibly taint and corrupt both the adherents of Judaism and the faith itself.[34] Her solution focuses upon the concept of holiness, notions of completeness and perfection, and efforts to eradicate pollution (both deliberate and inadvertent).[35] Some animals may be a source of this impurity.[36]

Other components of Jewish dogma may have been as comprehensible to Gentiles as they were to Jews themselves, and could be assimilated into a system of knowledge pertaining to foreign customs and ideologies. In some senses, similarity between Jews and Gentiles may have been greater than their differences.[37] Many of the methods used in the Graeco-Roman world to isolate or identify social and ethnic groups were simply not applicable to the Jewish community, especially in large, urban environments. Jews did not habitually wear different clothes, adopt distinctive hairstyles or necessarily converse or write in a different language.[38] Many would have spoken Greek as a common

(31)    Plut. *Quaest. Rom.* 268.
(32)    Douglas (1966), 54–72.
(33)    Douglas (1966), 56.
(34)    Douglas (1966), 61–2.
(35)    Douglas (1966), 63.
(36)    Neusner (1975), 21.
(37)    Cohen (1993), 1–45.
(38)    Cohen (1993), 8.

language. They did not possess distinctive names or occupations, and although they may have lived in neighbourhoods occupied by a predominant ethnic group, but it does not appear that *only* Jews inhabited these areas, nor they were solely confined to them. Philo referred to the division of the city of Alexandria into five districts. Two were inhabited by a Jewish majority.[39] At the same time, there certainly were distinct religious observances remarked on by outsiders, even if some of these might be shared by other cultures. Herodotus, for example, notes that Egyptians – not just Jews – practised circumcision,[40] even though Latin authors thought it peculiarly Jewish.[41] Tacitus maintained it was employed by Jews to keep themselves separate.[42] This physical statement of dissimilarity implies not just a display to outsiders, but a technique for recognizing each other. The only other absolute visual clue to a Jew's religion was if he were asked to make obeisance to a pagan deity and refused.[43]

Food, therefore, was the most palpable mark of Jewish identity.[44] I observed earlier that many authors chose to concentrate on the Jewish abstinence from pork. This, like circumcision, was also practised in Egyptian temples, at least according to Josephus,[45] but more widely it was greeted with a mixture of baffled incomprehension and scorn (although some writers, including Plutarch, did at least make some attempt to discover the origins of the taboo). Much of this has to do with attitudes towards this particular animal. Pork was ubiquitous, gracing both the tables of the wealthy and the poor.[46] Latin authors, in particular, seemed to have derived particular pleasure in satirizing the Jewish taboo. Their mockery was not especially malicious. Sometimes it was sheer delight in wordplay and punning. Plutarch, in his life of Cicero, recalled the latter's play on words when conducting the case against Verres, the *propraetor* of Sicily. The joke hinged upon the name of the disgraced senator and the Latin word for boar, and a connection with Jewish dietary

(39)   Philo *In Flacc.* 55.
(40)   Hdt. II.36; 104. Also Goldstein (1939), 356. Initially, he states that they were the only proponents of this custom, but later modifies this, stating that other races, such as the Ethiopians and the Colchians, adopted the practice, with the Phoenicians and the Syrians of Palestine following suit.
(41)   Hor. *Sat.* I, 9:70. Mart. *Epig.* VII,30:5. Mart. *Epig.* VII,35:3–4. Mart. *Epig.* VII, 82:6.
(42)   Tac. *Hist.* V, 5:2.
(43)   See Athanassiadi and Frede (2001). A conference on this topic was held at the University of Exeter 17–20 July 2006. A publication is forthcoming.
(44)   Zuesse (1974), 21.
(45)   Joseph *Ap.* 2.282.
(46)   See Dalby (2003), 268–9; Wilkins and Hill (2006), 147–149 for the importance of the pig in Graeco-Roman culture.

practice.[47] In a similar vein, Macrobius reports the witticism of Augustus, who is alleged to have commented that it would have been preferable to have been Herod's pig than his son. This jest manages to encapsulate the ruthlessness of Herod, the longevity of a pig in Jewish society and a similarity between the Greek for 'son' (*huios*) and 'pig' (*hus*).[48] Other observations were less benign. Juvenal's disgust at Jewish customs is evident throughout. He too remarks upon how, in a Jewish community, a pig may survive until old age. Elsewhere, he implies that the Jewish mentality likens the eating of pork to the act of human cannibalism.[49] Philo notes the scoffing of Caligula at the practice, although his jest seems to have been born of a cruel and sardonic wit, and a desire to belittle the Jewish delegation from Alexandria, rather than from any deep anti-Semitism.[50] It was noted, both by Jews themselves and by others, that the dietary laws could be taken extremely seriously. Sextus Empiricus refers to Jews who preferred to perish rather than consume pork.[51] During the Alexandrian pogroms, suspected Jewesses were coerced into tasting pork in order to test their religious affiliation.[52]

There was much ignorance of Jewish practice. This is illustrated by those who sought to amalgamate the observance of the Sabbath with the custom of fasting.[53] So frequent is the assertion that some scholars question whether in fact Jews *did* fast on the Sabbath in antiquity.[54] There is no real undertaking in these texts to engage with the reasons behind the pork prohibition. It was viewed as an opportunity to exploit ethnic stereotypes. A few did make efforts to be more scholarly and less partisan. Epictetus remarks that Jewish food laws were just one manifestation of naturally conflicting dietary ideologies that existed between races.[55] Plutarch also attempted a sober appraisal, and took the analysis a little further. In the *Table Talk*, he ponders whether the genesis of the pork prohibition lay in feelings of reverence towards the pig

(47)   Plut. *Cic.* 7.5.
(48)   Macrob. *Sat.* 2.4.11.
(49)   Juv. *Sat.* XIV, 98. A similar remark is made by Galen; Gal. *de al. fac.* K663. Galen's observation pertains to the apparent similarity of human flesh to that of swine, rather than adopting a censorious attitude towards pork eating.
(50)   Philo *Leg.* 361–362.
(51)   Sext. Emp. *Pyr.* III, 23.
(52)   Philo *In Flacc.* 94.
(53)   Suet. *Aug.* 76. Also, Martial's reference to the stench of the breath of female observers of the Sabbath (*ieiunia sabbatariarum*); *Epig.* IV.4.
(54)   See Michael (1924), 122–4.
(55)   Epictetus apud Arr. *Epict. diss.* I,11:12–13;22:4.

by the Jewish people, or in an attitude of disgust and abhorrence. If the beast
were venerated, then this would be no more surprising than the attitude of
the Egyptians towards some animals.[56] However, it was not so much that the
animal was worshipped as a divinity in itself by the Jews; rather it was afforded
respect because the pig, by snuffling in the soil with its snout, gave birth to
the art of ploughing. This was regarded as a plausible explanation, even more
so given that the Egyptians were prone to revering animals for reasons that
were far less worthy.[57] And, after all, if the Jews had hated the pig, it would
logically have followed that they would have attempted to harm or kill the
animal. The contrary argument was also presented: that Jews abominated the
beast because it was physically filthy, and carried disease.[58]

Plutarch was not the only observer to make a connection between the
pig and leprosy. Tacitus makes a remark in similar vein.[59] They attempted to
engage with the notion of 'uncleanness' but concentrated instead on simple,
tangible dirt: the pig's appearance, its environment and its diet. Tacitus also
links the Jews themselves to bodily filth and disease. The concept of spiritual
pollution is largely ignored or disregarded. Tacitus is often thought the most
vituperative Latin critic. The crux of his argument is that the practices and
customs of the Jews were an inversion of those of the Romans. Circumcision,
and the insistence upon separate foods and dining apart from Gentiles, was
interpreted as a form of hostile cultural secession.

The division of Jews and Gentiles into two distinct and unitary groups
is misleading. Just as Gentiles cannot be regarded as a single homogeneous
entity, so Jews may be subdivided, each community with its own stance on
dietary matters. From Josephus we learn of the Pharisees, the Sadducees and
the Essenes.[60] There often occurred segregation between these sects. The
Essenes were particularly austere and only ate together (in fact, they ate no
other food than the one common meal they shared on a daily basis). Similarly,
the Pharisees ate apart from the rest. If we seek to assert the importance of
dietary restriction as a technique for achieving social cohesion, we have to

(56)   Plut. *Quaest. conviv.* IV.5. 669–670.
(57)   Plut. *Quaest. conviv.* IV.5. 669–670. He refers to the Egyptian deification of the blind
       field mouse, owing to that culture's reverence for the dark over the light.
(58)   Plut. *Quaest. conviv.* IV.5. 670F–671. Leprosy is a major concern of *Leviticus* 13 (perhaps
       reflecting a greater prevalence of the disease in the Middle East than in Greece or Rome).
       See Manchester (1984), 167–169.
(59)   Tac. *Hist.* V.4.2.
(60)   Joseph. *Vit.* 10–11. For the nature of these sects, see Baumgarten (1973), 93–110.

accept that this may occur on a micro level but for larger groups it may prove a source of division.

If some Jews were more enthusiastic about dietary laws than others, so others within the Diaspora might have been prepared to ignore the whole thing. Perhaps the laws were undesirable and unworkable in the context of displacement and integration and were rapidly discarded, or more acknowledged in the spirit than the deed.[61] Assimilation militated against dietary separatism.[62] But unless we assume Gentile references to Jewish practices were baseless, then lapses cannot have been too frequent.[63]

There are few references to how Jews arranged their specific requirements *vis-à-vis* food slaughter and preparation. An exception is the report by Josephus of a decree, passed in the first century BC in Sardis, stating that the officials of the city market should ensure that food that was suitable for Jewish consumption was made available.[64] As Zeev's commentary on this passage makes clear, not only does this seem to indicate that in Sardis Jews were adhering to their dietary laws, but the necessary procedures to procure the special foods were enshrined in local law.[65] The decree does not describe these procedures in any detail. Presumably, they concerned both the types of animal and the way they were slaughtered. Perhaps the decree was meant to ensure that the restrictions upon activity imposed by Sabbath observance were taken into account. This would mean that food would be available on a particular day (or perhaps that food would be held back, so that others would not take food in their absence). Of course, this decree is but one instance of pro-Jewish dietary legislation by the Roman authorities, and we are unable to infer from this that such consideration was an empire-wide phenomenon. Perhaps the Jews of Sardis felt the need to lobby actively for such rights to appear as law, as they were unable to achieve their ends informally. Other communities may have arranged things differently.

It is also possible that a service industry may have built up around the provision of these special items. A passage in the elder Pliny seems to point to a special type of *garum* manufactured to take into account Jewish requirements.

(61)    Barclay (1996), 435.
(62)    Barclay (1996), 435.
(63)    It is possible that Greek and Latin texts may have exaggerated the assiduousness of Jewish adherence to their dietary laws if the author was writing in an anti-Semitic vein, and felt that such hyperbole better served to illustrate his motif of Jewish separatism.
(64)    Joseph. *AJ* XIV, 261.
(65)    Zeev (1998), 224. Also Sanders (1992), 215–216; 520, note 12.

Unfortunately, Pliny becomes rather confused and believes that such sauce is made from fish without scales.[66] He appears to be under the misapprehension that the only types of fish that Jews were permitted to consume were precisely those species forbidden them. Nonetheless, it indicates some sort of provision to manufacture foods especially for Jewish consumption, though whether by Jews or Gentiles is unclear. Pliny's observation may be entirely mistaken but, significantly, he is willing to acknowledge that there was rather more to the dietary laws than mere pork abstention.

Such was the power of the connection of the latter with Judaism that it seems that any person or group that chose not to eat this meat (for whatever reason) ran the risk of being thought a Jew. A passage in a letter of Seneca reveals how he himself had encountered such a problem during his early life, when his vegetarianism was associated with foreign rites, at the time viewed with suspicion by the administration of Tiberius.[67] In AD 19, Tiberius ordered the expulsion of the Jews from Rome, for reasons that are still not entirely evident.[68] There was a real danger of being forced into exile if one were mistaken for a Jew. The rationale for the expulsion appears to have been the result of a period of general cultural anxiety rather than pointed anti-Semitism, whether of the citizen body or the authorities. After all, Egyptian cults were subject to a similar decree, as were astrologers. If we are to believe the accounts of Dio and Josephus, the impetus for the crackdown was the success of Jewish proselytism.[69] Seneca's remarks about the dangers of religious misidentification should be seen in the context of a period of persecution of many foreign cults, not just Judaism. However, Jewish regulations bore at least a superficial resemblance to the protocols of other 'inferior' nations, particularly the Syrians and the despised Egyptians. In popular imagination, it is easy to imagine how the Jews became amalgamated with the Egyptians and other eastern races in an indistinguishable blur of animal idolatry, genital mutilation and dietary phobias.

Jewish religious laws were a complex, well-defined system for maintaining a state of purity, a state that was necessary to assert their distinctive and unique

(66)   Plin. *HN* XXXI,95.
(67)   Sen. *Ep.* CVIII, 22.
(68)   Suet. *Tib.* 36.; Cass. Dio LVII,18; Joseph. *AJ* XVIII, 81ff.; Tac. *Ann.* II,85. See Gruen (2002), 29–36. for a discussion of the possible reasons for this expulsion. Merrill (1919), 365–372.The Jews were subject to numerous exclusion orders in the first century. They were expelled for a period during the reign of Claudius; Suet. *Claud.* 25. Also Slingerland (1992),127–144.
(69)   Gruen rejects this position; 31.

relationship with God. Dietary purity went hand-in-hand with circumcision, ritual bathing, observance of the Sabbath, temporary fasting, and prayer. In the eyes of outsiders, their dietary discipline rendered the gastronomic life of the Jews a barren wasteland: annoyingly problematic and unspeakably dour. It made the procurement and preparation of meals laborious and time-consuming, and was prohibited completely on the Sabbath.[70] It excluded one of the most popular and widespread of meats. They seemed to negate one of the most important functions of food in the ancient world, a means of social cohesion. Of course, as has already been noted, the act of eating within Jewish culture did promote social unity, but given the existence of ideologically diverse sects within Judaism, such cohesion could only have occurred at family level, or between members of the same sect. The connections that were formed by a shared pattern of eating within Judaism were not cross-cultural. The laws simultaneously united and repelled (outsiders).

In this sense, the Jewish culinary experience serves to reinforce, several times each day, cultural and religious selfhood. The act of satisfying each pang of hunger was a regular reminder of the urge to achieve absolute purity. Each mouthful was an *aide-mémoire* to worship God and to follow His commandments. Dietary laws gave others the view that Jewish identity was stubborn and contrary. Jewish piety was looked upon as primitive superstition, their self-perceived holy status seen as arrogance, their refusal to accept other gods or acknowledge the divinity of the emperor as both unreasonable and seditious. Their diet was a pointless and illogical anomaly.

Jewish dietary laws may be viewed as almost the epitome of the way in which dietary restrictions influenced the way in which ancient identity was constructed. A strict regime of behavioural rules ensured that purity was not compromised. In this sense, they were a set of regulations with a positive end. For Gentiles, however, one of the most prominent features of these laws was the sense of negation and self-denial. The laws seemed designed to squeeze every last drop of pleasure out of life. All they did was talk of the foods one was forbidden to eat. Food was treated not as a possible source of delectation, but as a potential threat. An unguarded moment could lead to a mouthful of an illicit food. One swallow could result in irrevocable contamination. To someone like Tacitus, these food laws were an atrocity perpetrated against Roman sensibilities; a hostile act that wilfully shut out the world, and enjoined

(70)    Augustus did make provision that Jewish observance of the Sabbath did not hinder their ability to receive the grain dole; Philo *Leg.* 158. Also Gruen (2002), 28–29.

the Jews to retreat into a cultural bubble. And yet, this isolationism was not absolute, for Jews actively participated in the economic life of the city. The Jews were an enigma to a culture that was relatively comfortable with the way radically diverse peoples could peacefully co-exist under the shelter of the umbrella of Roman authority.

CHAPTER SIX

# RESTRICTIONS UPON ALCOHOL

When we examine how alcohol was consumed in antiquity, it is important to bear in mind that it differed greatly from other, edible goods. It was not necessary to consume it to survive.[1] Its calorific and vitamin content rendered it a negligible source of nutrition.[2] It was a toxic substance that was used not to extinguish life but to enhance it. Lastly, it was a psychotropic material that could radically alter sensory perception.[3] Alcoholic beverages are a nonessential foodstuff,[4] whose absence from the diet would not be injurious to health.[5] Yet, they occupy a central position in many diverse cultures, both ancient and modern.[6] In some cases, alcohol is an essential accompaniment to meals – wines are chosen to complement specific foodstuffs – and *aperitifs* and *digestifs* serve to awaken the palate and aid the digestive process. This

(1)  Although it could be argued that, as with beer in the medieval period, alcoholic beverages were actually safer to drink than water.

(2)  Schmidt (1980), 25–40.

(3)  I accept that an alteration of mental and physical faculties was not an exclusive property of alcohol; the taboo surrounding the broad bean was sometimes attributed to its powers to interfere with corporeal functions, in particular the dreaming process. Also, numerous studies today have sought to link sugars and preservatives in food to the mental processes and behaviour of children.

(4)  The categorization of alcohol as a foodstuff may be problematic to some cultures, although rather less so to others. See Engs (1995), 228–229 for differences in drinking patterns between Northern and Southern Europe.

(5)  This is not to negate the medical studies that have found numerous heath benefits in drinking certain types of alcohol in moderation, merely to assert that its removal from diet would be unlikely to imperil life, or to pose a serious threat to health.

(6)  For variations in cultural attitudes to alcohol, see Mandelbaum (1965), 281–288 & 289–293. Also Douglas (1987).

model of gastronomic behaviour has escaped geographical restrictions and spread across the globe.

But alcohol can be taken without food, consumed for its own sake. The lowering of inhibitions that comes from drinking in a group promotes interaction and cohesion (or, sometimes, brawls and estrangement). It acts as social lubricant, easing feelings of awkwardness, introversion and insularity in a convivial atmosphere.[7] The rosy glow of intoxication provokes a certain egalitarianism among diverse social and cultural cohorts. Conversely, drinking may reinforce those hierarchies based around systems of inclusion and exclusion.[8] Some drinking traditions buttress group identity. In modern societies, one might instance initiation ceremonies of American college fraternities or stag and hen parties within British culture.[9] These could be compared to the orgiastic rites of the followers of Dionysus.[10] The ephemeral abandonment of moral principles permits acts of licentiousness and various forms of horseplay.

Anthropologists have seen the use of alcohol in modern Western societies, as a significant marker separating the worlds of work and leisure.[11] The strict, organized and hierarchical demeanour appropriate for work gives way to less formal modes. The American sociologist Joseph R. Gusfield employs the term 'keying' in order to describe this modification of behaviour.[12] The shift may involve a change of clothes, or a move to a different location which serves further to emphasize the distinction between the spheres. Hence the anxieties that arise over the minefield that is the office Christmas party, when alcohol and its effects invade the work environment.

(7)     See Gusfield in Douglas (1987), 78. Gusfield refers to this as 'cultural remission': 'the conventionalised relaxation of social controls over behaviour'. He goes on to suggest that alcohol permits greater freedom of word and deed, because if verbal and behavioural *faux-pas* occur, these may be blamed upon excessive alcohol intake: 'by shifting the burden of explaining embarrassing moments from reflection of the self to the effects of alcohol, drinking provides an excuse for lapses of responsibility, for unmannerly behaviour; for gaucheries, for immoral and improper actions', 79.

(8)     See Mars in Douglas (1987), 91–101, for the strictly controlled hierarchical drinking rituals of longshoremen in Newfoundland. These drinking arrangements, according to Mars, effectively control and strengthen the rules that govern who possesses greatest economic power within this industry.

(9)     Leemon (1972).

(10)    Burkert (1985), 161–167; Seaford (1981).

(11)    Gusfield in Douglas (1987), 73–90.

(12)    Gusfield in Douglas (1987), 79–81.

There are parallels between our relationship with alcohol and that of
the Graeco-Roman world. Not least our moral panic over its abuse, which
can be acute insofar as it pertains to the lower classes and new or unfamiliar
users such as young women or minors but edges towards toleration when the
drinker belongs to the élite. Our concerns often mask anxieties about social
mobility or shifts in the balance of economic power, and the potential threat to
patriarchal systems.[13] These arguments about the social effects of alcohol, who
has access to it and its potential significance for cultural and social mutation,
are not irrelevant to the way in which alcohol was used in antiquity. There are
striking similarities in both drinking customs and an awareness of the benefits
and dangers that it presented to the individual and to society as a whole.

Modern readers will understand the word alcohol to encompass a range
of distilled, fortified and fermented liquids. In a Graeco-Roman context, it
almost certainly signified wine. Wine was felt to be a characteristic of Graeco-
Roman civilization and was contrasted with intoxicants of less sophisticated
races such as the beer of Egyptians or Celts.[14] In Greek and Roman culture,
wine possessed a religious sanctity: production and ingestion were inextricably
linked with Dionysus/Bacchus.[15] Wine was regularly, although not invariably,
used as a religious libation.[16] Wine was central because grapes grew well in the
Mediterranean homeland. In the north, where the climate militated against
successful viticulture, the fermentation of grains gave rise to a different set of
habits and preconceptions.[17]

(13)     Garnsey (1999), 109.
(14)     See Forbes (1951), 281–285; 300. See Wilkins and Hill (2006), 131–132 for beer in Greek
         and Roman territories.
(15)     Of course, the fusion of wine with the rites of worship of a deity is not a phenomenon
         that was exclusive to Greco-Roman religions. Wine performs a pivotal function in the
         celebration of Communion within Christian worship, although in this context it has
         become transformed entirely into a symbolic element.
(16)     Perhaps the most notable recipients of wineless libations were the Eumenides. See
         Henrichs (1983), 87–100.
(17)     It has also been suggested that the relative lack of daylight in some of the countries of
         northern Europe (as compared with the sunnier climes of many Mediterranean lands)
         may also have some impact upon attitudes to alcohol (see Engs (1995), 230). This
         argument is not without its flaws. It proposes a model of drinking that defines countries
         or cultures as being essentially homogeneous in character. This definition ignores the
         many variations of drinking behaviour. For example, many countries that produce wine
         in sizeable quantities are not characterized as being populated by people who drink wine
         *and nothing else*. They may drink a wide variety of other alcoholic drinks, such as beer
         or spirits.

Although in the discussion which follows there are many instances of people counselling against excessive drinking, there is not a lot of hard evidence from ancient sources for the existence of acute or chronic alcoholism or deaths from liver or brain damage. Authors talk of crippling hangovers and the nausea that tended to follow extended drinking bouts, but evidence of more serious health problems is anecdotal at best. One may cite the tales of the potations of Alexander the Great; and the writings of Aristotle (or possibly pseudo-Aristotle) on wine and drunkenness are revealing. He talked of the incessant trembling of the drunkard, which he attributed to the cold, but which sounds more like *delirium tremens*.[18] This lack of information stems from both limits to ancient medical knowledge and the fact that the effects of alcoholism only become apparent after many years of heavy drinking. When lives were shorter than our own, death intervened before the symptoms were in evidence.[19]

The standing of wine in Greek culture was on of wholly enthusiastic acceptance. Scholars have asserted that all city states passed laws to control its use, and that Sparta prohibited it.[20] There is still some debate over whether there was an absolute prohibition in Sparta; Plutarch records that moderate drinking did take place at their collective mess meals.[21] Excess was frowned upon and helots (the Spartan slave class) were made to over-indulge so that their intoxication might serve as a lesson to Spartiate youth.[22] It is clear that Plutarch is talking of restraint, not a complete embargo. Xenophon, too, comments that while there was some control exercised over the intake of wine in Sparta, there was no absolute interdiction. He notes other Greek states (and his implication is that Sparta is *not* included) made strenuous endeavours to regulate access to wine by females, or ensured it was watered down for them.[23] In Sparta, drunkenness was severely condemned and it was the compulsion to drink, so noticeable in Athenian *symposia*, that is removed from the Spartan

(18)    Arist. *Pr.* III,26.
(19)    Some, such as Garnsey, would argue that the zenith of mortality was infancy; see Garnsey (1999), 52. Such deaths were equally common among rich as well as poor.
(20)    Lissarrague (1990), 5.
(21)    Plut, *Inst. Lac.*237. The phrase 'pinontes... metrōs' does not make explicit that it was wine that was being consumed, but it seems likely that this was meant. Plutarch's pro-Spartan bias and his chronological distance from the period he describes makes this an unreliable source for the actual drinking habits of the Spartans.
(22)    Plut, *Inst. Lac.* 239A.
(23)    Xen. *Lac* I.3. This comment is misleading; most wine consumed in the Greek world was watered down. See 208; 221–222.

dining experience.[24] Though Sparta was in general authoritarian in its social mores, the matter of wine was left to individual judgement. Since intoxication denoted moral and physical feebleness and was a source of great shame (as it often is in many modern Mediterranean cultures), it was assumed that collective disapproval would be discouragement enough.

Greeks in general recognized that wine presented a physiological as well as moral threat. Philo thought undiluted wine noxious.[25] The term *akratos* (unmixed) is of great significance in Greek (although to a lesser extent in Roman) culture. Greeks thought wine without water both dangerous and the custom among the savage and the barbarous.[26] The level of dilution was, if the texts reflect actual practice, carefully considered when arranging a symposiastic gathering.[27] It is intriguing that Athenaeus remarks that the use of the adjective *akratos* could also be used with reference to water (presumably meaning 'water unmixed with wine', rather than vice-versa).[28] Galen could point to the properties of wine that could bring cheer to men's souls and aid the digestive process, and yet, at the same time, could emphasize wine's potential dangers by remarking on Homeric warnings against its excessive ingestion, and noting Plato's proposed restrictions upon its use.[29]

Latin literature, too, is replete with ambivalent musings about the fruits of the vine, with endless paeans to its role in the delights of the *convivium* sharply contrasted with castigation of excess. The intoxicated debauchery of statesmen in antiquity is a familiar *topos*, with a strong emphasis upon the putative relationship between drunkenness and tyrannical or aberrant behaviour.[30] Opinion was not inevitably polarized between the two extremes of consumption and abstinence. Those who warned of the dangers were just as aware of its benefits. The essential question was one of vigilance and control.

(24)   Xen. *Lac* V.4. It is debateable whether there were drastic differences between the Spartan and Athenian drinking experiences. Davidson calls attention to a remark of Diogenes the Cynic in a fragment of Aristotle's *Rhetoric* that makes an ironic comparison between the messes of Sparta and the bars of Athens; Arist. *Rhet.* 3.10.4, 1411a24. Davidson (1997a), 392.

(25)   Philo *Noah* 147.

(26)   Although neat wine *was* used for libations to the gods; Wilkins and Hill (2006), 176.

(27)   Plut. *Quaest. conviv.* III.9.

(28)   Fr. 94 in Ath. *Deip.* 44b.

(29)   Gal. *QAM.* ; Hom. *Od.* xxi. 293–8; Pl. *Leg.* II, 666a–c.

(30)   Suet. *Tib.* 42; *Claud.* 33; Plut. *Alex.*; Cic. *Phil.* II. Also *SHA*: *Verus* 10.9; *M. Ant.* 9.3. Often, the virtuous ruler is characterized by his abstemiousness in both food and drink; Suet. *Iul.* 53; *Aug.* 87. See Scott (1929), 133–141; MacUrdy (1930), 294–297; McKinlay (1939), 51–61.

What seems strange is that such control does not seem to have been imposed from above but was achieved by self-regulation.

Drinking practices were not uniform across the Graeco-Roman world, nor did they remain static over time. The Greek *symposium* was, as far as we are aware, an exclusively male affair (with the exception of the female entertainment), with drinking following the meal and in a well-worn sequence of poetry recitation and composition, the singing of songs, and games of manual dexterity (such as *kottabos*).[31] Some form of snack or dessert (*tragêmata*), perhaps nuts or fruits, most likely accompanied the sympotic drinking.[32] The Romans seem less likely to have excluded women (although they may not have been permitted to drink wine) and drinking would seem to have occurred with the meal rather than after it.

As in our own day, total abstainers were often reckoned puritanical and joyless.[33] Plutarch thought them tedious and mediocre company: 'Teetotallers are offensive people (*aedeis*): they make better nursemaids than symposiarchs.'[34] Horace thought that abstainers should not be permitted to compose poetry as they lacked the necessary inspiration that wine may provide.[35] This is not to say that water was stigmatized, merely that those who drank it in preference to wine were sometimes viewed as bland and fatuous. And water itself was not without its dangers. Vitruvius may have lauded it as indispensable to human existence but he knew that not all water tasted the same nor possessed identical properties.[36] Some springs were pleasant to drink from, from others seeped liquid death.[37] He catalogued those that were acid, or caused intoxication and stupidity, or even made one's teeth fall out.[38] Athenaeus, too, was keen to make a survey of the diverse types of water and their various attributes.[39] Cicero, in the *Pro Caelio*, alludes to water that was

(31)    See Pellizer (1990), 181 for presence of women at Greek symposia.
(32)    It seems unlikely that no drinking at all would have taken place during eating.
(33)    Plaut. *Aul.* 572–574. Megadorus' invitation to Euclio to drink water is rebuffed by the latter, who insists that he is only drinking water. This is met with incredulity. For modern temperance, see Carlson (1998), 659–691; Schneider (1978), 361–372.
(34)    Plut. *Quaest. conviv.* I.iv.2. Dodds (1933),101.
(35)    Hor. *Epist.* i.19.8–9. See Smith (1984),255–71; McKinlay (1946), 161–7. See also Cratinus, *Anth. Pal.*xiii.29, Kock i.74, Ath. *Deip.* II,39c: ' You who drink water can never produce anything good (hudōr de pinōn kreston ouden an tekois)'. See Wilkins (2000), 243–256.
(36)    Vitr. *De arch.* VIII, I, 1.
(37)    Vitr. *De arch.* VIII, III, 1;VIII, III, 15–17.
(38)    Vitr. *De arch.* VIII,III,17–23.
(39)    Ath. *Deip.* 40–46.

being used by prostitutes to wash themselves after sexual intercourse.[40] It may be imprudent to extrapolate from this that water was somehow commonly connected in the popular imagination with both prostitution and intimate hygiene, although it is plausible that water was thought particularly, but not exclusively, associated with washing (especially before meals) and the experience of the baths.[41] Thus, water may have been thought both good and useful – and in religion it was used to achieve spiritual cleanliness in some rites of purification – but not something to drink.[42]

Even those who escape direct censure for sobriety are damned with faint praise. Seneca discusses in his letter on drunkenness the problems of drink, citing the notorious examples of Alexander the Great and Mark Antony, but generally comes down on the side of those who indulge. Zeno is quoted as claiming no secrets may be entrusted to a drunkard, but Seneca counters that with the remark, 'how many soldiers who are not always sober have been entrusted by a general or a captain or a centurion with messages which might not be divulged.'[43] He cites the admirable example of Lucius Piso:

> the director of Public Safety at Rome, [who] was drunk from the very time of his appointment. He used to spend the greater part of the night at banquets, and would sleep until noon. That was the way he spent his morning hours. Nevertheless, he applied himself most diligently to his official duties, which included the guardianship of the city. Even the sainted Augustus trusted him with secret orders when he placed him in command of Thrace.

Then he refers to an infamous drunkard, Tillius Cimber, part of the conspiracy to assassinate Julius Caesar, and compares him with the water-drinking Cassius. It is unclear whether Seneca is attempting to link sobriety with heroic tyrannicide or treachery; either way, Cassius makes an unlikely poster-boy

(40)   Cic. *Cael.* 34. Also Bruun (1997), 364–73; Butrica (1999a), 136–9, Butrica (1999b), 336. In the latter, the author points to 'a special connection between prostitutes and the use of water. This is the word *aquariolus*, defined in the *OLD* as "a servant who supplied washing-water for prostitutes" ',336.

(41)   I say 'not exclusively' as I am aware that the rural and urban attitudes to water in the Roman world may have been very different. If the urban experience of water centred around the baths, beyond the limits of the city, water may have been conceptualized in terms of agriculture, particularly the irrigation of crops.

(42)   Burkert (1985), 70–73; Parker (1983), 226ff.

(43)   Sen. *Ep.* 83.

for the moral benefits of drinking water. These water-drinkers hail from no particular socio-political or economic class. They are geographically diffuse, as Athenaeus' catalogue of noted water imbibers makes evident.[44] It was purported (by himself) that the orator Demosthenes was a water-drinker, at least temporarily.[45] The behaviour of a fellow-orator, Demades, a whoring drunk, is contrasted with the sober and diligent Demosthenes.[46]

It should come as little surprise that it was supposed that Pythagoras abstained from wine.[47] Iamblichus said those aspiring to the highest levels of Pythagorean philosophy were urged to leave off drink.[48] Diogenes Laertius was equivocal. He asserted that Pythagoreans believed that for mental and physical well-being one should drink only water,[49] but went on to mention how Pythagoras was reputed to have never consumed wine during the day.[50] The inference that he drank at other times is unsupported in other texts.

These attitudes to alcohol were not absolute. Time and context would determine their application. A temporary interdiction might often be obligatory or desirable, for instance during a religious festival. Plutarch, discussing the origins of the Homeric description of salt as divine, remarked that religious considerations might require temporary abstinence from particular practices.[51] These included laughter, childbirth and the drinking of wine.[52] Alcohol was sometimes thought acceptable to some members of the community but not to others. Aristophanes' *Thesmophoriazusae* dealt extensively with male concerns about female drinking. Aelian claimed that there was a law in Massilia (Marseilles) prohibiting women from drinking wine.[53] He also alluded to a similarly stringent item of Roman legislation that forbade wine to women and slaves, and men between adolescence and the age of thirty-five.[54] The elder Pliny listed famous examples of draconian measures taken against women if they were suspected of having drunk too much (or indeed any) wine.[55] And

---

(44)   Ath. *Deip.* 44b–d.
(45)   Ath. *Deip.* 44c.
(46)   Fr. III.2 Baiter-Sauppe in Ath. *Deip.* 44f.
(47)   Stob. *Flor.* XVIII.33.
(48)   Iambl. *VP* 15.69; 17.78; 24.107–8.
(49)   Diog. Laert. *Pythag.* VIII.13
(50)   Diog. Laert. *Pythag.* VIII.19.
(51)   Plut. *Quaest. conviv.* V.10
(52)   Plut. *Quaest. conviv.* V.10.684–885.
(53)   Ael. *VH.* 2.38.
(54)   Ael. *VH.* 2.38.
(55)   Plin. *HN* XIV.xiv.89–91.

Plato saw a need to regulate access to this dangerous substance.[56] He was particularly concerned about its effects upon youth.

The drinking habits of the lower orders were of especial moment. The modern historian Nicholas Purcell comments on the increase in the number of taverns and bars in Rome during the imperial period, but notes that it was 'in the very late Republic and Empire that low-class establishments selling wine attract the systematic attention of the authorities'.[57] James Davidson addresses similar concerns about the growth of the phenomenon of the tavern (*kapêleion*) within the context of Greek urban space.[58] He posits that such was the level of anxiety about these establishments that they had been banned in Athens.[59]

Davidson makes a sharp distinction between mass and élite drinking practices within Greek culture. John Wilkins, in contrast, sees the lines as more blurred. He perceives a broad spectrum of plausible contexts within which drinking could take place. The *symposium* should not necessarily be regarded as the exclusive preserve of the élite. It seems that alcoholic aspirations could be downwardly as well as upwardly mobile. Suetonius refers to the young Nero, disguised with cap or wig, enjoying nocturnal rambles through the streets of Rome, drinking and carousing in taverns.[60] It is plausible that aristocrats may have found the *milieu* of patrician revelry stifling and sterile, and would have enjoyed the occasional opportunity to rough it in disreputable company.[61] Edwards offers an alternative explanation:

---

(56)     Pl. *Leg.* 2.666a3–b3. Also Belfiore (1986), 421–437.

(57)     Purcell (1985), 15. Purcell does not make it clear that this attention is because of drunken behaviour or something else (congregation of the poor, excessive noise, fire hazard). However, as he goes on to refer to Ammianus Marcellinus' view of Rome as a seat of inebriated misbehaviour, we must assume that he means the former. His footnote ( note 70) seems to indicate that there was some lawlessness, even during the early Empire, owing to wine prices and distribution.

(58)     Davidson (1997a), 392–395. Davidson (1997b), 53–60.

(59)     Davidson (1997a), 393. Davidson posits that such prohibition had as much to do with a fear on the part of oligarchic government of gatherings of the people as it was of drunkenness. As he notes: 'An oligarchic regime may simply have shared the prejudices of Theopompus and Isocrates against the practice of drinking in bars, seeing a ban as a measure against decadence and vulgarity, but it is not hard to think of more practical considerations too. Any kind of gathering of the lower classes was threatening to a newly installed oligarchy'; 395.

(60)     Suet. *Ner.* 26.

(61)     These sorts of activities may have been a fairly commonplace occurrence amongst groups of aristocratic youths. See Eyben (1993), 107–112. In fact, Eyben suggests that Nero provided a role model for such activities.

that Nero's behaviour was a way of consciously drawing attention to the fact that he was playing a role.[62]

Turning to how the consumption of wine was regulated, it was either by self-regulation or external judicial sanctions. By self-regulation I mean the way individuals or groups could choose to manage their own drinking. For this to take place, there had to be a recognition that excess was undesirable, and that it was the ultimate responsibility (even the duty) of oneself (or one's peers) to limit consumption. In Greek sympotic culture, control fell to the *symposiarch*. It is not certain how dictatorial this role was. In the *Symposium*, Plato tells of the guests, physically and mentally enfeebled by the rigours of the previous night's carousing, reaching a collective agreement to reduce their intake on the next day.[63] Plutarch has several observations to make upon the nature of the role.[64] One of his interlocutors, Crato, seeks to define the *symposiarch* as being of an exceptionally convivial nature, neither easily prey to intoxication, nor hesitant in enthusiastically participating in the drinking.[65] He goes on to stress that it is absolutely vital that he who controls the drinking must be aware that each man may react to drink in a different way. He must be able to direct proceedings so that drunkenness does not descend too quickly and thus sour the occasion.[66] There existed a fragile boundary between a pleasant *soirée* and a drunken debauch. And yet, it would be foolish to deny that a compelling reason for drinking alcohol is to experience some level of intoxication. Greek idealism may have seen wine as a subtle relaxant, lubricating the wheels of social interaction, but there is no denying that the ability of wine, taken in excess, to alter consciousness radically and break down inhibitions must have proved a powerful draw, at least to some. After all, the end result of the

(62)   Edwards (1993), 193. This argument seems unconvincing. Nero's nocturnal activities in the streets and taverns were carried out in disguise. The only people to know his true identity would have been his companions or bodyguards. Any other encounter would surely have resulted in the emperor being mistaken for someone who was "low". If this were not the case, the activity would have been largely pointless. Eyben (1993), however, suggests Nero's activities provided an impetus for other youths to behave in a similar way. Cass. Dio LXI.8; Tac. *Ann.* XIII.25.

(63)   Pl. *Symp.* 176e.

(64)   Plut. *Qaest. conviv.* I.4 *What sort of a man the symposiarch must be.* Interestingly, again on this occasion of a literary *symposium*, although a *symposiarch* is appointed (Plutarch appoints himself), the guests are invited to set their own pace of drinking ;I,4,620B. This seems to belie Lissarrague's assertion that the dictates of the *symposiarch* required absolute obedience; Lissarrague (1990), 8.

(65)   Plut. *Quaest. conviv.* I.4,620C.

(66)   Plut. *Quaest. conviv.* I.4,620E–621B.

*symposium* was a state of intoxication. Wine was frequently viewed as a source of poetic stimulation, lifting the poet from the level of the mundane to that of the divine.[67]

Even within the context of an élite male group, consisting of those with free access to wine, who were judged able to estimate how much they could safely imbibe, restraints were considered necessary to ensure that an abundance did not produce anarchy, violence or uncontrollable sexual urges. If this sounds implausible, one has only to read the accounts of inebriated symposiasts who imagine themselves to be in a ship at sea.[68] Plutarch reasoned that symposiarchical management involved matching guests, arranging a mixture of games, songs and discussion, lubricated with just the right amount of wine to produce a harmonious whole. The consumption of food prior to (and perhaps concomitant with) drinking may have slowed the effects of alcohol, but perhaps the most significant element of regulation during the *symposium* was dilution.[69] Plutarch treats this briefly, attempting to establish the most useful rate.[70] Three parts water to one of wine was thought too weak, while two to one was too potent. The ideal was three parts water to two of wine.[71]

The atmosphere of the Roman *convivium* seems more relaxed, with a more nebulous concept of what was expected. There was less emphasis on third-party control, greater freedom allowed the individual.[72] The two principal differences between the *convivium* and the *symposium* were that the first permitted the presence of women as guests (not merely as servants or entertainment), and that it integrated the activity of drinking with the meal. The result may have been that the quintessential Roman experience saw less drunkenness thanks to the mitigating factors of food and the beneficent presence of women. Aelian remarks that it was unusual for women to be partial to wine.[73] It is not clear if he means women drinkers were unusual because their sex did not like wine or that their fancy was inhibited by the many cultural and legislative barriers

(67)    Wilkins (2000), 218.

(68)    Pind. fr. 124a Snell; Timaeus 566F 149 in Ath. *Deip.* 37b–d. See Slater (1976), 161–70; Wilkins (2000), 224, 238–241.

(69)    Wine dilution may not always have been inspired by this ideological stance. After all, there are sound economic reasons for the practice, not least in that it enabled those engaged in selling it to achieve a greater profit.

(70)    Plut. *Quaest. conviv.* III.9,657B. See also Wilkins (2000),216–218.

(71)    Plut. *Quaest. conviv.* III.9,657C–D.

(72)    Dunbabin (2003), 22.

(73)    Ael. *VH* 2.41.

placed in their way. However, caution should be exercised over these tales of draconian measures, particularly in the Latin sources.[74] They may have formed part of the literary *topos* that sought to envisage early Roman society as unblemished by later alien 'decadent' practices. These stern morality tales refashion history with a hefty dose of misogyny, restoring distorted social hierarchies and eradicating foreign cultural contamination.

There are many accounts of extreme drinking practices among the Roman élite. The emperor often set the tone of aristocratic drinking, as described by Pliny:

> Nero once again outdid everyone as befits an emperor, by paying a million sesterces for a single wine-bowl. Let us not forget how seriously the Emperor and Father of the Fatherland took his drink.

When Cicero castigated Mark Antony for vomiting while hungover as he conducted public business, it was noted that he had been drinking at a wedding. Cicero's family was not without blame, however, as Pliny recounts:

> Tergilla records that Cicero, the son of Marcus Cicero, was in the habit of knocking back six litres of wine in succession. Once, when he was drunk, he threw his goblet at Marcus Agrippa, as drunks do. No doubt Cicero was trying to beat Mark Antony's (his father's murderer) own drinking records. Cicero even went so far as to write a book about his own drinking.[75]

Pliny reported a trend during the reign of Tiberius for both drinking upon an empty stomach and drinking before the start of the meal.[76] This seems more an attempt to achieve early intoxication than an example of the *aperitif*. It indicates that Roman drinking was not always implacably wedded to eating. Juvenal scathingly referred to a woman drinking on an empty stomach to quench her thirst and stimulate her appetite. Pliny the Elder describes a typical drinking party taking place in the baths:[77]

(74)   Wilkins makes a connection between the limits placed upon female drinking and Roman sumptuary legislation relating to female expenditure on clothing and jewellery; Wilkins and Hill (2006), 179.
(75)   Plin. *HN* XXVII.vii.20; XIV.xxviii.147; Cic. *Phil.* II. 25.63.
(76)   Plin. *HN* XIV.xxvii.143.
(77)   Juv. VI. 427–428; Plin. *HN* XIV.xxviii.139.

Some of these drinkers are carefully boiled in the bath, until they are carried out unconscious. Others never get to the dinner table, because they can't get into their tunics. Still panting and naked, they clutch an enormous wine vessel as though to demonstrate their strength. Then they drink this to the dregs, only to vomit it all up and start drinking again. They do this a second and a third time as though they were born for the purpose of wasting wine.

Inevitably, external cultural influences, changing fashions and immigrant influx produced transformations in behaviour as well as a coalescence of Greek and Roman drinking practices. For instance, there did exist a form of drinking party (*comissatio*) within Roman culture, although it may have been a more marginalized phenomenon than its Greek counterpart.[78] It is not clear whether the many references to enthusiastic drinking in Latin poetry were within the context of the *convivium* or the *comissatio*. Martial's quaffing,[79] and Horace's boast that he could outdrink the Thracian bacchants,[80] may point to social occasions in which drinking, rather than eating, were the focus, or they may be instances of literary self-presentation, in which heroic toping becomes part of a strategy of self-aggrandisement. The 'sophisticated' Greek ideal seems debased as it is subsumed by Roman cultural hegemony. Perhaps the problem lies not so much in a divergence of attitudes but the idealized way in which these forms were presented in literature. Perhaps the carefully regulated *symposium* was just a literary fiction, an aspiration. It may be profitable, when considering Roman practice, to think about the way in which it would have been altered by other cultural influences. It seems plausible that some sort of hybridization may have occurred, resulting in a bastardized phenomenon, neither *symposium* nor *convivium*, but something else entirely.

It is useful to return to the previously discussed notion of 'keying'.[81] This indicated the way in which rituals and settings connected with drinking serve to separate modes of behaviour, and to delineate the boundaries between work and leisure. This helps our understanding the ritualized and hermetically sealed world of symposiastic drinking. Male peer-bonding and the loosening

(78)     Dunbabin (2003), 21. She notes the emulation by the *comissatio* of the form of the *symposium*, with the *magister* or *arbiter bibendi* taking over the role of *symposiarch*. See also Faas (1994), 87–101.
(79)     Mart. *Epig.* I,27.
(80)     Hor. *Carm.* II, vii.
(81)     See page 85.

of inhibitions occurs within a tightly controlled context. The rules of the *symposium* took temporary precedence over cultural norms. Transient licence was allowed to the participants. The world of everyday 'non-drinking' life did not intersect with that of the *symposium*. Although drunkenness might result, it was confined to the *andron* (that part of the Greek house reserved for men) – unless it spilled into the public sphere by means of the *komos* (a procession through the streets of masked revellers). This separation of real life from bouts of drinking may explain why Cicero thought Mark Antony culpable: because when he was drunk he failed in his public duties; he mingled the two spheres, patrician decorum was compromised. Excessive drinking, even drunkenness, was not necessarily condemned, but criticized if it transgressed social norms. Sobriety in a *symposium* or *comissatio* was inappropriate, but drunkenness was unacceptable in the public realm.

In Greek and Roman texts there is often marked distrust of life's visceral pleasures. They were thought harmful to public order and the fabric of aristocratic society. Athenian young men could guzzle fish and wine, and could lust after unsuitable youths, the cream of Roman aristocracy could whore, drench themselves in exotic scent and drink away their inheritance, but commentators saw such patterns of behaviour as a cancer relentlessly eating away at society. But most of what was written was by the élite and for the élite; immorality or self-destruction among the lower orders was of far less importance. The modern historian Catherine Edwards nicely observes that the nobility, by choosing to squander vast sums of money upon prostitutes, gambling and drinking, helped wealth to flow downwards.[82]

Wilkins has suggested that it is unhelpful to think of élite and mass drinking customs as being polar opposites within Greek culture. Aristocrats could wallow in taverns, while the general population could seek to emulate élite forms of sympotic behaviour. Wilkins' argument is strengthened by the assumed familiarity of the audience with sympotic activities in Athenian comedy.[83] If it were a distant and unfamiliar preserve of a rarefied clique, surely any comic potential would be wasted upon a diverse non-aristocratic crowd? Nick Fisher highlights one defect of this position: the audience has gained its knowledge not from *symposia* themselves, but from repeated exposure to dramatic representations of them.[84] James Davidson notes that

(82)   Edwards (1993), 180.
(83)   Wilkins (2000), 208.
(84)   Fisher (2000), 348.

the implementation of any rigid division between rich and poor drinking may have been a stratagem of the élite to prevent the contamination of their culture by the lower orders.[85] Public bars and taverns were an obvious *milieu* for proletarian drinking, but one should also consider the occasions of public feasting and festivals. Bars (*kapeloi*), in Athens at least, were particularly associated with public drinking, particularly for women and the lower classes.[86] Many similar establishments have been uncovered in Roman towns such as Ostia and Pompeii. The satirist Juvenal describes the disreputable clientele of such an establishment:

> Look for him in a *popina* [tavern], Caesar, because you'll find him there lying with a hit-man, in the company of sailors, thieves and fugitives, among hangmen, coffin makers, a drunken castrated priest and his abandoned drums. Freedom prevails there, everyone drinks from the same cup, no one goes to bed on his own and no one sits at a separate table.[87]

One may speculate as to whether the drinking habits of the masses were subject to the checks and balances characteristic of the élite. It is debatable whether they would have chosen to separate the worlds of drinking and non-drinking in a similar fashion. The division between the spheres of work and leisure referred to by the sociologist Joseph R. Gusfield can be matched by another partition (and he is aware of this), between males and females, noted by Mary Douglas. Males consume their drink in a predominantly male work context, not in the home.[88] If this model could be applied to the drinking culture of the masses in antiquity, many of whom would surely have been engaged in some form of manual labour, then we may speculate that drinking was not separated from work, but from the domestic sphere. There is still a gender division, but otherwise this arrangement is the inverse of élite behaviour. The affluent drink domestically (although in Greece not with families) but not publicly, and the poor do the opposite. There appears to exist no opprobrium for the latter group about drinking in the public sphere. All come together for drinking at festivals. Given this lack of a sense of shame, and

(85)   Davidson (1997b), 58.
(86)   Wilkins (2000), 167. Also see pages 217–219.
(87)   Davidson (1997b), 54; Juv. VIII.171–8.
(88)   Douglas (1987), 8.

the absence of a meaningful ideology of work/leisure partition, restrictions upon alcohol were rarely self-imposed (excepting through poverty).[89] Curbs on drinking most likely came from external judicial procedures. We have noted some form of legal sanction to prevent Roman women and children drinking alcohol, and it seems likely that slave access to it was tightly controlled by owners.[90] Perhaps legislation existed merely to deal with the crimes that may have resulted from excessive drinking – vandalism, violence, adultery – rather than acting as prevention.[91] Those who would argue against restrictions imposed on wine drinking by the poor may point to an edict of Aurelian in the late third century AD that proposed to add wine to the foods (which also included oil, bread and pork) distributed to the poor of Rome.[92]

The control of alcohol intake was undoubtedly of vital importance to both Greek and Roman societies. Alcoholic drinks were one of the markers of cultural identity that served to reinforce hierarchical structures of power, and indicated terms of inclusion and exclusion. Wine drinking marked the civilized nations as being different and superior to the barbarians who swilled beer. Internally, the type of wine that was consumed separated the affluent from the poor. The manner in which it was imbibed could, in spite of Wilkins' reservations, act in a similar way. However, such were the powers of alcohol that it could also make possible the dissolution of hierarchical boundaries: wine as the great social leveller. Alcohol is always a double-edged sword. Aristocrats could dabble in the pleasures of the masses, but even with their supposed moral superiority risked loosing the genie of egalitarianism from the bottle, thereby contaminating themselves. Intoxication could result in

(89)  The whole notion of a 'work versus leisure' ideology is problematic in itself, and I accept that the ancients adopted no coherent line upon the matter. Work (and perhaps here it is best defined as 'manual labour) could be viewed as both ennobling and pleasing to the gods, or debasing and suitable only for pack animals and slaves. Such attitudes could, of course, shift over time, and, undoubtedly, greater economic prosperity (and hence a greater number of slaves) would have altered attitudes. For a discussion of this in a Greek context, see Balme (1984), 140–52. For Edwards (1993), the tension lies not between work and leisure *per se* but with the virtues or vices that are perceived to result from these activities (173–206). It should be emphasized that these concerns very much emanated from the *élite* segment of the Graeco-Roman world.

(90)  For example, Cato *Agr.* LVII for wine rations for slaves. For restrictions on female drinking, see pages 223–224.

(91)  It seems more likely that, like sumptuary legislation, any controls would have stemmed from a desire to stop gatherings of people who may have harboured dissident cultural or political views. Compare this with Davidson on Athenian bars; Davidson (1997a), 215–216.

(92)  SHA *Aurel.* 48.1.

aspirations to the divine, but also a descent into the realms of bestiality. It could liberate one's true identity by loosening the shackles of self-awareness and customary morality, but it could also destroy the self by casting it adrift from its cultural and moral foundations. Only control could ensure that the individual (and the state) did not freefall into anarchy. Much of what is available from the sources point to a concern with the effects of alcohol on the ruling élite, and a sentiment that regulation lay very much with the individual. This anti-authoritarian stance is quite startling, and surprising in its scant regard for the behaviour of the majority.

Much of what we read about the restriction on alcohol in antiquity points to concerns about the correct division of society, but also an intense awareness of the fragility of the bonds that act as society's glue. Alcohol is an agent that may easily dissolve that adhesion. Its destructive and beneficial powers were accorded equal recognition. Like a wild animal straining at its tether, an admiration for its beauty was tempered by the knowledge of its destructive force should it ever break free from its confinement.

CHAPTER SEVEN

# STATE CONTROL OF FOOD: SPARTAN
# DIET AND ROMAN SUMPTUARY LAWS

The existence of sumptuary legislation presumes a tension between the government and the citizen. It suggests a definite and tangible impetus towards luxury, among at least a section of the population, that should be checked or controlled. Sumptuary laws, designed to restrain and regulate the exercise of hedonistic impulses, are moralistic in tone, authoritarian in nature. They view human nature through the prism of pessimism: man as an an animal in thrall to corporeal appetites, a gluttonous, rutting beast, dazzled and ensnared by baubles and trinkets. The tradition of sumptuary legislation is still alive in contemporary societies. It may not take the form of edicts about clothing, or class-based tables of what may or may not be consumed, but the state is still concerned with citizens' behaviour inasmuch as it impacts on public health or the administration of justice. The unspoken rationale for these laws, however, will often be an amalgam of distrust of sensual pleasure and a fear of social destabilization. The sociologist and historian of sumptuary laws, Alan Hunt, notes their two defining features. They were an active measure to preserve and strengthen the *status quo*, and they often possess a gender bias, although not always, as expected, directed against the female sex.[1]

In this chapter I discuss such legislation in two ancient societies: the Greek city-state of Sparta and the Roman republic and early empire. In both, anti-luxury laws tap into deep-rooted insecurities and aim straight for the very heart of identity, whether acting as a form of sticking-plaster pressed

(1)     Hunt (1996), xii–xiii.

ineffectually over the gaping arterial wound of perceived eastern decadence in republican Rome, or a bulwark against the perceived evils of encroaching foreign customs in Sparta. They seek to protect and nurture some perceived form of national and cultural identity. These concerns about luxury and its effects arose at times of social, religious and political upheaval. The adversary is change. Sumptuary legislation is a conservative beast and sees in alteration not progress but decay and degeneration. It aims to preserve the *status quo*, or to force society into reverse gear.[2]

The historian of racism in antiquity, Benjamin Isaac, sees Greek thought as more isolationist than Roman although he suggests that xenophobic sentiments found in literature were often belied by political practice.[3] He cites a fragment of Xenophanes, the fifth-century BC philosopher and poet from the Ionian city of Colophon, in the *Deipnosophistae* of Athenaeus that refers to the Colophonians becoming degenerate and corrupted owing to their contact with the Lydians (of whom the most celebrated was King Croesus).[4] He also reminds us of Plato's assertion that the ideal location of a city should not be too close to the coast, as this would encourage the import of foreign goods.[5] The ocean may act as a conduit for corruption, alien ideologies, immigration (and escape), and luxury. However, an isolationist policy could only go so far in preserving moral integrity; the peril was not just external. Sumptuary legislation was as often used to combat social change from within, to ensure social and hierarchical boundaries were not blurred or dissolved.[6]

The definition of what constitutes a luxury and what is essential may depend on cultural and economic contexts as well as personal views. While some luxuries endure through time (the value placed upon gems and precious metals, works of art or rare foods), some pertain to particular circumstances.[7] Many today will be perplexed at the veneration for fish displayed in fifth-

(2)     See Isaac (2004), 239.
(3)     See Isaac (2004), 240. However, this still remains of interest owing to the ideological preoccupation with cultural separation, clearly at odds with actual practice (if Isaac's assertion is correct).
(4)     Xenophanes F3B (Diels Kranz) =F3 (West) = (Lesher); Ath. *Deip.*526a; Isaac (2004), 239. Wilkins (2000), 263.
(5)     Pl. *Leg.* 706; Isaac (2004), 241.
(6)     This is not entirely true. Sparta's own form of anti-luxury legislation (at least as expressed in the texts of Xenophon and Plutarch) sought to achieve a society in which the economic and social differences between Spartiates were deliberately de-emphasized.
(7)     The same items could be regarded as both an essential and a luxury, depending upon how it is used. A mineral element may have an intrinsic value, or it may be perform a useful function within a technological context. Sekora (1977).

century Athens and the dying years of the Roman republic (although, as fish stocks dwindle, we may soon share their sentiments). In an era of widespread poverty, profligacy was thought morally doubtful, but at other times an impulse towards possessing rare and precious objects had both an aesthetic and economic rationale. In modern societies, consumer spending on non-essentials is one of the many factors ensuring the buoyancy of market economies.[8]

A common feature of goods seen as luxuries is their association with physical pleasure.[9] Another is exoticism: the perfume, the spice, or the remarkable plant must be sourced from abroad. Luxury is also frequently characterized as feminine. In antiquity, the quality of femininity possessed negative connotations, associated with physical weakness and lack of moral fibre: an inability to practise self-control.[10] Developing from this, it was also deemed tyrannical, the subject of the feminine whims and self-indulgence of oriental despots. The control of female social behaviour is inextricably linked with sumptuary legislation. Female emancipation, like the love of expensive food or a predilection for silk, may be regarded as a sign of weakness, a chink in the state's inviolable moral defences.

The notion of luxury in antiquity simultaneously tapped into many of the most problematic and sensitive areas of ancient cultural identity: race, gender and class. The development of luxury and its transmission between cultures, and the many attempts made to suppress impulses towards luxurious behaviour, may be regarded as a symbolic embodiment of the cultural anxieties that afflicted the Graeco-Roman world. The territorial growth of nations, increases in personal and collective wealth and population migrations forced unfamiliar peoples and cultures into close proximity and compelled many to embark upon a process of self-examination. It obliged them to define their own character, to identify those qualities they saw as essential. The focus of this chapter will be the ways in which luxury and the intermittent war against it manifested itself in dietary matters. This will often mean food, rather than

(8)     And it is noteworthy that in these types of capitalist societies, sumptuary legislation does not exist.

(9)     It could be argued, as I have attempted to do so in the case of foodstuffs, that the epithet 'luxury' may also be usefully applied to items that may be physically insubstantial in nature, for example music, or perhaps literature or philosophy that is not preserved as written text for posterity.

(10)    See Dench, 121–146 in Wyke (1998). Book 12 of the *Deipnosophistae* contains numerous examples of eastern tyrants, whose decadence is characterized by effeminacy, use of cosmetics and exotic clothing.

alcohol, as surprisingly, this dangerous liquid was subject to far fewer state controls than may be supposed (see the preceding chapter).

Food may at first appear an unlikely candidate for the sobriquet luxury. There is nothing more essential to man's survival. But, in reality, it may well be the most apposite. Expenditure of money and effort upon things like statues and buildings was justified on the grounds of permanence. But what pleasure was more ephemeral, more transitory than a meal? To spend great wealth on food, something quickly consumed, scarcely remembered and ultimately excreted, was indeed the ultimate luxury.

Originally, sumptuary laws seem to have been aimed predominantly at funeral activities. Alan Hunt views this as being linked with the control of women.[11] This seems to be borne out by Solon's legislation in Athens, which placed limits on both female freedom of expression and movement and on female lamentation at funerals. The words of Dryden's translation of Plutarch have it thus: [12]

> He [Solon] regulated the walks, feasts, and mourning of the women and took away everything that was either unbecoming or immodest; when they walked abroad, no more than three articles of dress were allowed them; an obol's worth of meat and drink; and no basket above a cubit high; and at night they were not to go about unless in a chariot with a torch before them. Mourners tearing themselves to raise pity, and set wailings, and at one man's funeral to lament for another, he forbade. To offer an ox at the grave was not permitted, nor to bury above three pieces of dress with the body, or visit the tombs of any besides their own family, unless at the very funeral; most of which are likewise forbidden by our laws, but this is further added in ours, that those that are convicted of extravagance in their mournings are to be punished as soft and effeminate by the censors of women.

An inscription found on an island not far from Athens, dated to the fifth century BC and thought to be a copy of a Solonic law, provides limits for expenditure and expressions of grief at burials. There is more emphasis placed upon costume

(11)    Hunt (1996), 18.
(12)    Plut. *Sol*.21.4. It is dubious how accurate Plutarch's account of Solonian legislation is, given the chronological distance from the events he is describing. Mills (1984), 255–265; Seaford (1994), 74–86; Dryden's translation is at http://classics.mit.edu/Plutarch/solon. html (accessed 3 February 2010).

than food, and Hunt notes that, despite a similar concern with funeral practices, this was a significant difference between Greek and Roman legislation.[13]

Certain writers used the theme of sumptuary legislation as a springboard to explore issues of cultural identity. In the austerity these laws promoted, they saw a way of offering a critique of their own societies. Scholars are divided on the motives behind such lawmaking. Was there a genuine moral impetus? Was it to preserve the unity of the Roman patrician class of the first and second centuries BC, divided by strife, with members competing for prestige and status?[14] Could they have been, as for example the Lex Oppia of 215 BC, a reaction to specific events (in that case, the defeat at Cannae in the Second Punic War)?[15] Or was the legislation, as some have characterized the laws enacted by Demetrius of Phaleron in Athens at the beginning of the fourth century BC, little more than an exercise in public relations designed to quieten the jealousies and resentments of the lower orders?[16]

Both our chosen examples of sumptuary regulation (Sparta and Rome) attracted the attention of many writers in the first and second centuries AD and beyond. They sought to make explicit connections between the two societies. They often seem to have written to a specific agenda. They look back at the past with a strong nostalgia and use their explorations (and recreations) of the past to make pointed criticism of what they see as the decadence of Rome. The historical and the imaginary merge as they redefine and reinterpret the past and reinvent the present. Greeks, in particular, look at Greek ethnic identity and draw parallels between the past glories of a free Hellas and the realities of present Roman subjugation.

Archaic Sparta under the authority of Lycurgus sought through radical social measures to create an abstemious and militaristic society, purged of extraneous wealth and extravagant personal behaviour and isolated from external influence.[17] As related by Xenophon (and much later by Plutarch), the Spartan constitution offers an example (perhaps *par excellence*) of mortal dread of indulgence and luxury lying at the heart of government and social

(13)    Hunt (1996), 19. The Twelve Tables of the Romans contained a provision for the curtailment of extravagant funeral arrangements (Table X). It is possible that such legislature may have been influenced by the Solonic code; Cic. *De leg.* ii, 64. Also Seaford (1994), 75.
(14)    Crawford (1992), 75–76.
(15)    Dupont (1992), 146.
(16)    Green (1990), 47.
(17)    For Spartan dietary legislations, see David (1978), 486–495; Figueira (1984), 87–109; Fisher (1988), 26–50.

mores. This anxiety governed how they reared their children, the clothes they wore, their economy, and how they ate. At least, this is what we are told by certain texts.[18] Our principal sources are writers distant in time and place from their subject, unable as outsiders, by their own admission, to gain access to the territory. So their accuracy, and indeed their disinterest, are in question. Xenophon and Plutarch both had their own agendas. Xenophon's comments probably reflect his concerns about the Athens of his own day (the early fourth century BC). In the case of Plutarch, it seems clear from his other writings (particularly the *Lives* and the essays of the *Moralia*) that his view of Sparta dovetailed into his concerns with moral behaviour, the problems of luxury, and restricted diet. Plutarch's own Greek heritage, and the question of what it was to be Greek in a Roman-dominated world, act as filters. It is a view that idealizes the past. It presents a vision of a strong, disciplined military state that existed long before Rome, which itself built on and emulated this earlier example.

Later discussions of Sparta give the impression that the Lycurgan reforms displayed a collective anxiety about alien contamination.[19] The creation of the constitution was attributed to Lycurgus, the lawgiver.[20] Biographical details are vague, with confusion about his activities and even as to when he lived.[21] In a sense, such matters are inconsequential, sufficient to note that he was assumed to have lived before or at the same time as Homer and the Spartan constitution was thought to have the weighty respectability of age.[22] Plutarch's *Life* makes Lycurgus almost a heroic archetype, personifying and crystallizing a process of social and political mutation that may have, in reality, been a gradual and piecemeal process of constitutional and legislative reform, taking place over many years.[23]

(18)    For discussion of Spartan social laws, particularly pertaining to food and drink, see Fisher (1988), 26–50. I hesitate to label the Spartan laws as 'sumptuary legislation'. They are not the same as what was enacted in republican Rome (although there appear to be certain similarities).

(19)    It is difficult to state with any great certainty how far the reality of daily existence for the Spartiate corresponded with the details preserved in texts such as Xenophon's. The legislation may have been little more than a hopelessly idealistic and aspirational set of rules.

(20)    Xen. *Lac.* i. 2; Plut. *Lyc.* For Lycurgus, see Hammond (1950), 42–64; Forrest (1963), 157–179; Hodkinson (1983) and (2000); Rawson (1969).

(21)    Plut. *Lyc.* i.1.

(22)    Xen. *Lac.* x. 8. Xenophon dates Lycurgus to the time of the Heracleidae.

(23)    Rawson (1969), 9: 'In reality it seems likely that Sparta underwent a fundamental reform or series of reforms about the early seventh century BC rather than at any of the variable but earlier dates given us for Lycurgus'.

What exactly was intended by Spartan moral/sumptuary legislation?[24] The impetus seems to have been an attempt to forge a society that was martial in character, perpetually ready for war. To this end, it needed to be pared back to bare necessities and to be essentially communist in form: to remove every source of inequality. Equality, however, only for the Spartiates (the *homoioi*). Strict hierarchical divisions still applied to those under Spartan subjection: the *perioikoi* and the helots. Land ownership was re-organized to remove the evils both of excessive wealth and penury.[25] Individualism was firmly discouraged, and the lifestyle of a Spartiate was firmly regimented.

The common mess-meal, *syssitia*, has been regarded by some as the principal symbol of Spartan cultural and political identity.[26] Membership was apparently a mandatory part of being a citizen.[27] This system of communal eating was unusual in the Greek world but was not unique. Its origin is to some extent confused, with doubt cast on whether Lycurgus was responsible or not.[28] Similar arrangements could be found in Crete, Miletus, Thebes and Carthage.[29] Scholars such as Humfrey Michell believed that Sparta adopted their eating practices from Crete. A Cretan derivation is absent from Xenophon and Plutarch, although the latter's *Life* claimed that Lycurgus visited Crete and took inspiration from some, although not all, of the laws he found there.[30]

Communal eating seems to have been poly-functional. Plutarch asserted that it removed the desire and the opportunity for indulging in soft and decadent behaviour. It laid open one's eating habits to the scrutiny of one's peers.[31] Texts suggest that it was not universally popular; Plutarch thought the wealthier citizens resented it the most.[32] In spite of government attempts

(24) For more on this, see Hodkinson (2000), 200–235; MacDowell (1986), 111–122.
(25) Plut. *Lyc.* viii. 1–2.
(26) Hodkinson (2000), 217.
(27) Arist. *Pol.* 1271a 26–37; MacDowell (1986), 211.
(28) Michell (1952) writes: 'The Spartans themselves of course attributed, quite erroneously, the foundation of these messes to Lycurgus, who made a law', 281. Athenaeus, in his discussion of Spartan dietary behaviour in Book 4, does not comment upon the origins of this custom, although he has a good deal to say about the nature of the mess meals. He does comment, at 141f, that the Spartans eventually abandoned this life and embraced luxury. However, later, in Book 6, the philosopher Pontianus asserts that Lycurgus would allow nothing luxurious into his state (233a–b).
(29) Michell (1952), 286.
(30) Plut. *Lyc.* IV.i. Polybius rejects any similarity between the Cretan and Spartan constitution; Polyb.VI, 47.
(31) Plut. *Lyc.* x.3.
(32) Plut. *Lyc.* XII.

to achieve an egalitarian society, therefore, a form of economic hierarchy persisted. Indeed, this economic imbalance was judged by Aristotle the crucial defect of the mess-meal.[33] Unlike the Cretan system which was subsidized by the state, Spartan messes demanded a fixed minimum contribution of food each month from every member.[34] This dietary levy meant, according to Aristotle, the exclusion of poorer citizens. Even within the *syssitia*, equality was conspicuous by its absence. Seating was graduated by rank, and wealth allowed a member to go beyond the provision of the minimum contribution to provide extra food donations.[35] These may have been behind the most infamous element of Spartan diet: the black broth.[36] This dish of pork and blood, notorious for its foulness, was supposed to have been a Spartiate staple. It seems likely that, in spite of the popular notion of the uniformity of Spartan diet – its blandness and its communal nature – meals were more varied in content and context. Athenaeus, for instance, has a long excursus on Spartan meals and feasting including a fragment from Cratinus about the festival called *Kopis*, 'Cleaver'.[37] The feast, open to foreigners, involved the sacrifice of goats.[38] At the meal was also served a cake (*phusikillon*), as well as cheese, sausages, and a dessert consisting of dried figs, dried beans and green beans.[39] This was certainly not lavish, indeed meagre by comparison with other Greek states, but it was hardly starvation. Austerity, it seems, was relative. Cratinus also remarked that at Cleaver, 'in the public lounges sausages hang nailed to the walls for the old men to bite off with their teeth.'

As an ideological utopia, with a constitution that was orally transmitted not written, Sparta could be all things to all people. It offered a model vague enough for later writers to overlay their own emphases and concerns. Sparta, as a paragon of military virtue and order, was a source of imitation and comparison for the nascent Roman state. And both fell victim to corruption brought by wealth and foreign values. Points of comparison between Sparta and Rome were a frequent theme of many second-century writers.[40]

(33)    Arist. *Pol.* 1271A.26–37.
(34)    Plut. *Lyc.* XII.
(35)    Hodkinson (2000), 253–254.
(36)    Plut. *Lyc.* XII.7; *Inst. Lac.* 236F.
(37)    Ath. *Deip.* 138e.
(38)    This goes against what Plutarch says about Sparta being closed to foreigners, unless the foreigners referred to by Athenaeus are the limited number of diplomats to whom Holladay (1977) refers, 119–120.
(39)    Ath. *Deip.* IV.138f–139b.
(40)    See Rawson (1969), 107–115.

Correspondences between their eating habits were also noted, especially the ways that access to and spending on food was controlled.[41] Hence Valerius Maximus' comparison of the severity of Lycurgan Sparta with that of earlier Rome.[42]

In Rome, we possess many accounts of successive sumptuary laws that were proposed and passed (occasionally repealed) for a period of approximately two centuries from the beginning of the second century BC until the reign of Nero.[43] They chronicle what seems a Canute-like attempt to control lavish personal expenditure by the aristocracy. The laws offer moralizing authors an opportunity to compare and contrast, and they often used food as both a metaphor and an instance of the perceived decay of society.[44] It would be largely pointless to fix a date for the start of this activity (as if social changes may be fixed absolutely in moments of time) but Romans themselves liked to do so. They did not always agree. Often, the destruction of Carthage in 146 BC was regarded as significant.[45] The removal of this potent political rival led to introspection and subsequent decadence.[46] In the *Deipnosophistae*, the Roman host Larensis cites Lucullus as being the first man to introduce such extravagances.[47] Livy takes us back further to 187 BC with the influx of foreign luxury goods into Rome following the victories in the east of Gnaeus Manlius Vulso.[48] It does however reveal the tacit assumption that indolence bred iniquity. The elimination of a target for the exercise of Roman martial virtue inevitably led to a dissipation of this energy.[49] Ironically, victory may mean eventual defeat. These attempts to locate this 'immorality' in a single external source (the removal of Carthage as a focus for Rome's energy), and

(41)     Ael. *VH*. 3.34. It is unclear to which law Aelian is referring here.
(42)     Val. Max. II.6. See Skidmore (1996).
(43)     From Livy, Aulus Gellius and Macrobius.
(44)     Gowers (1993), 21; Macrob. *Sat*. 3.17.9.
(45)     Polyb. VI.57; Val. Max. IX.1.3; Vell. Pat. II.i. 1–2.
(46)     Levick (1982), 53. And yet, the theme of Romans being contaminated and corrupted by foreign customs is ubiquitous in Latin literature; Isaac (2004), 242. In a sense, Roman culture is in a no-win situation. It is perceived that 'Roman virtues' only manifest themselves in war and conquest (which involves foreign contact and thus potential contamination). Success in the theatre of war leads to indolence and decadence. Isaac notes that, in a twist to the argument, contamination may flow in both directions, citing a passage in Strabo (7.3.7) that suggests that Romans taint other peoples with luxurious habits and vices; 242.
(47)     Ath. *Deip*. 274e–f. For Lucullus' extravagant dining habits, see Plut. *Lucull*. xxxix–xli.
(48)     Livy XXXIX. vi. 3–9.
(49)     Vell. Pat. II. I. 1.

very often to the acts of individuals, ignore that sumptuary legislation may be traced back much further. Livy tells of the attempted repeal in 195 BC of the Lex Oppia, passed twenty years previously, which placed restrictions upon female behaviour.[50]

Our principal sources for the legislation are Aulus Gellius and, much later, Macrobius.[51] Gellius maintains that early Roman austerity was produced by a combination of custom and law;[52] laws which sought to control the amount of expenditure spent by private citizens on dining, entertainment and clothing, and types of food consumed. His first example is the Lex Fannia of 161 BC which tried to limit expenditure on meals to no more than one hundred and twenty *asses* (excluding vegetables, bread and wine),[53] and stipulated that any wine served should not be of foreign origin.[54] If Athenaeus is to be believed, this law was ineffectual.[55] His second was the Lex Licinia (date uncertain) which restricted the daily intake of dried meat and salted goods while permitting fruits, vegetables and wine *ad libitum*.[56]

Evidence suggests that such laws were either ignored or greeted with hostility. There is a reference in Valerius Maximus (the sole one to this incident) where a tribune, Duronius, is expelled from the senate (probably in 97 BC) by the censors M. Antonius and L. Flaccus for revoking a law to cap the amount that could be spent on banquets.[57] The Lex Cornelia of Sulla in 81 BC was an effort to reinforce earlier laws. Strangely, its provisions, if reported correctly (by Macrobius; Gellius passes it over with little comment), appear counterproductive. It proposed lowering prices of luxurious commodities, not raising them. Thus, more people could afford them.[58] Macrobius thought the law useless. However, its purpose may have been to widen the availability of these goods. The very property that makes these items attractive – their exclusivity

(50)    Livy XXXIV. I. 8. The chief defender of the Oppian law, Cato the Elder, was himself portrayed as an archetype of the frugal Roman statesman. See Crawford (1992), 75–76; Culham (2004), 146.
(51)    Livy's account is closest temporally to the event; Gellius and (especially) Macrobius are chronologically distant, casting some doubt on the accuracy of their data.
(52)    Gell. *NA* II. xxiv. 1.
(53)    See Rosivach (2006), 1–15.
(54)    Gell. *NA* II. xxiv. 3–4. See Rosivach (2006), 3, note 9 for a discrepancy between Gellius and Macrobius over the amount. Gellius has the price limit for the dinner, Macrobius for each diner. Rosivach believes Macrobius must be mistaken.
(55)    Ath. *Deip*. VI. 274e–f.
(56)    Gell. *NA* II. xxiv. 7–10
(57)    Val. Max. II.9.5.
(58)    Macrob. *Sat*. III. 17. 11. Also Aubert in Flower (2004), 169.

– is diluted and tarnished. Witness, in our own culture, how long-haul air travel, champagne, caviar, and designer clothing have become accessible to the masses to the chagrin of the élite. This suggests an alternative motive for such laws: limiting competition between members of the aristocracy.

The emphasis on dining in Sulla's laws may have less to do with concern for the nation's soul and more to restrict the opportunities afforded by aristocratic dinner parties to plot, intrigue and subvert – all in secret. Macrobius notes that, as a pre-emptive strike, it was ordered that dinners be eaten with open doors.[59] This is a little reminiscent of the laws enacted by the Spartan regime many centuries before.[60] Valerius Maximus also makes reference to this habit of the ancients of eating *al fresco*.[61] The meals they took, he said, were plain and simple.

The Sullan legislation was followed in 78 BC by the Lex Aemilia, that sought to regulate not the expenditure on dinners, but the type of food that could be bought.[62] A law a few years later, the Lex Antia, was concerned with the dining behaviour of magistrates. To credit the much later account of Macrobius, the law, though never repealed, was generally ignored by a population thoroughly imbued with the vices of extravagance. Such was its ineffectiveness that its sponsor, Antius Restio, was reported never afterwards to have dined outside his house for fear of witnessing the public's disregard.[63]

Julius Caesar also weighed in with sumptuary enactments of his own. Suetonius writes:

> He imposed duties on foreign wares. He denied the use of litters and the wearing of scarlet robes or pearls to all except those of a designated position and age, and on set days. In particular he enforced the laws against extravagance, setting watchmen in various parts of the market, to seize and bring to him dainties which were exposed for sale in violation of the law; and sometimes he sent his lictors and soldiers to take from a dining-room any articles which had escaped the vigilance of his watchmen, even after they had been served.

(59)   John of Salisbury 8.7 (731d); Macrob. *Sat.* III. 17. 1
(60)   Xen. *Lac.* V.2.
(61)   Val. Max. II.5.
(62)   Gell. *NA* II. xxiv. 12.
(63)   Macrob. *Sat.* III. 17.13.

It is unclear whether he was more interested in punishing these acts of culinary villainy or ensuring that laws were strictly upheld.[64] His reputed parsimony may have had something to do with it. Suetonius writes of his punctilious dining habits, and of the unfortunate baker punished for serving guests different types of bread, graded according to the status of the guest.[65]

While there is a brief reference to laws passed in this area by Augustus, few details were given by Suetonius.[66] Gellius suggested he proposed limiting the amount spent on food *per diem*, depending on whether it was a working or festival day.[67] The last substantial mention of sumptuary legislation in the texts comes from the reign of Tiberius.[68] Suetonius made reference to measures to enforce frugality, including market price regulation by the senate, and restrictions on the sale of goods in cook-shops and eating-houses. He claimed that Tiberius set an example by his own frugality. The serving of leftovers at formal banquets was not unusual.[69] Gellius talked of a reference by Ateius Capito to a law passed either by Augustus or Tiberius (Gellius is unsure which) that raised the amount that might be spent on dinners on various festal days from three hundred sesterces to two thousand. The legislation appears to acknowledge that the state was fighting a losing battle against the increasing personal expenditure of the aristocracy.

Tacitus addressed this issue in greater detail. In his view, extravagance was a significant concern. In AD 22, Tiberius vetoed sumptuary legislation on the grounds that it would be a humiliating loss of face for the emperor to fail to enforce a law routinely ignored. The alternative, successful enforcement, would mean humbling some of the most illustrious citizens. To Tiberius, neither was acceptable.[70] With this in mind, a letter was sent to the senate, explaining the imperial position. The scale of the problem was acknowledged, with Tiberius asking the best place to start: villas, slaves, personal wealth, clothing?[71] He speaks of past laws, including those enacted by Augustus, which are useless and forgotten. For Tiberius coercion was ineffectual. The

(64)    Suet. *Iul.* 43.
(65)    Suet. *Iul.* 48.
(66)    Suet. *Aug.* 34.
(67)    Gell. *NA* II. xxiv.13.
(68)    There is a brief mention by Suetonius of sumptuary laws passed by Nero, restricting the type of foodstuffs that could be sold in wine shops to green vegetables and dried beans; Suet: *Ner.* 16.
(69)    Suet. *Tib.* 34.
(70)    Tac. *Ann.* III. lii–lv.
(71)    Tac. *Ann.* III. liii. Food appears not to have been an issue.

only way to achieve austerity was through personal effort.[72] He blamed
this moral laxity on the extent of the empire; these problems did not exist
(or, at least, were far less serious) when Rome was a smaller territory. He
urged self-restraint upon the population, in effect washing his hands of the
matter. At the end of this passage, Tacitus offered a rather strange summary.
Extravagance, he said, 'gradually went out of fashion' as a result of this imperial
announcement.[73] The culmination came with Vespasian. Tacitus ascribed the
change to both the personal example of this thrifty emperor and to an influx
into the senate of men from the colonies and provinces that brought with
them good household habits.[74] This Tacitean conclusion may have contained
a good deal of irony.[75]

This was hardly the end of luxury in the Roman world. Curbs upon
patrician spending were always doomed to failure.[76] Nonetheless, Tacitus'
comments shed some light upon Roman notions of luxury. He uses Tiberius
as a mouthpiece to express conservative anxieties about wealth, social identity
and ethnicity, here touching on traditional motifs in Latin literature. He
emphasizes the importance of self-control. In this instance, one is reminded
of how the Greeks used self-imposed controls upon sympotic drinking. Again,
the old notion of the contamination of Roman morals by foreign wealth and
customs rears its head. Of course, there is never the slightest suggestion that
a remedy might be the return of all plundered goods to their original owners
and the cession of all conquered territories. Tiberius claimed, said Tacitus,
that political expansion was the cause of moral decay. How do we reconcile
this with the Virgilian mission to civilize others? This paradox seems to lie at
the heart of Roman anxieties about identity. That which defines them – their
military prowess and the extent of their empire – may be the very thing that
eventually conspires to destroy them.

The writers under scrutiny track the social, economic and cultural changes
that occur within the Roman world over a number of centuries. Livy's
account of Cato's challenge to those wishing to repeal the Lex Oppia in 195
BC, written during the reign of Augustus, looked back to the earliest days,
when the pressure of foreign influence and wealth first made themselves felt.
The republic was a period of escalating conflict between aristocratic parties.

(72)   Tac. *Ann*. III. liv.
(73)   Tac. *Ann*. III. lv.
(74)   Tac. *Ann*. III. lv.
(75)   Edwards (1993), 202.
(76)   Crawford (1992), 75–76; Finley (1981), 188.

In relentless pursuit of personal glory and political supremacy, wealth was a weapon to be deployed. Extravagant dining was an opportunity to display largesse, to impress and perhaps intimidate. Simultaneously, it was something considered un-Roman; it could be a source of shame.

Extreme wealth became almost synonymous with the requirements of Roman citizenship (at least from the point of view of the élite). Virtue was no longer enough. The inflation of competition and the flood of wealth into society caused the meaning of affluence and poverty to be reset. At the end of the republic, it was no longer enough to be rich; one had to be very rich.

Tacitus' assertion that sumptuary legislation ceases to become an issue in the reign of Tiberius appears to bring the matter to a close. His observation that from the time of Vespasian, the example set by the ruler led to widespread frugality may have been true up to a point, but obviously he did not live to see the courts of Commodus or Elagabalus. Perhaps the reason that Tiberius gave up worrying about extravagance is that it no longer posed a threat. The use of wealth to gain power is largely irrelevant when all power lay with the emperor. Luxury was seen differently in the republic. Its political dimension was more potent. Under the empire, luxury itself becomes impotent. If it has any significance beyond the moral realm, it lies in enhancement of status.

But by some strange reversal, there was an incentive actually to understate the extent of one's wealth. This may have less to do with the example of the emperor's frugality, and more with a strategy for survival. Competing with the emperor in ostentatious spending was a dangerous game. And some emperors (Tiberius, Caligula and Nero to name but three) were not averse to having themselves named beneficiaries in the wills of the wealthy, then disposing of those individuals.

Dietary restriction within the context of ancient sumptuary legislation is a beast with many heads. It clearly has a moral impetus. An appeal to the stomach for restraint, an entreaty to the pleasures of culinary simplicity is both a means of appeasing nostalgia and a means of exercising social control. Archetypes of purer heroic societies appealed to conservative minds that saw social and political change as a path to destruction. These idealized portraits appeared repeatedly over the centuries in both Greek and Latin literature. In a world of complex and shifting identities, where multiculturalism was the norm, these strong moral certitudes were satisfying. Blame for the vices of modernity could be safely laid at the door of outsiders who brought the alien customs and afflictions concomitant with wealth. A love of spices or exotic fruits was a mnemonic for moral degeneracy, while a plain and unadorned diet represented a righteous nature or the food-as-fuel mentality of the warrior.

However, clearly there is something else going on. Dietary restriction is doing more than tapping into the rustic fantasies of Roman moralists or Greeks who feel the need to lose themselves in dreams of past glories. It seems to have been a tool to control social mobility and the exercise of power. Equally, it may be a voluntary method of self-definition, but it may also be used to define others. The fact that it repeatedly seems to fail may indicate as much the importance placed upon personal regulation of such things as a failure of the legislature.

Although notionally targeted at all society, sumptuary laws inevitably most affect the wealthy. It is they who are both able to travel abroad, and who possess the resources to procure rare and expensive items. For Spartans, even this was prohibited. The indulgence of self-expression through food was limited to the élite. The poor were politically impotent, so simply did not matter. Their form of dietary restriction was hunger. If it defined their identity in any way, it is simply to mark them out as poor and lacking choice. Sumptuary legislation would have made no difference to those for whom a simple diet was not a moral choice but a daily fact.

CHAPTER EIGHT

# GLUTTONY VERSUS ABSTINENCE:
# THE TYRANT AND THE SAINT

As we have seen, a restricted diet often helped ancient peoples make sense of the world around them. Culinary demarcation lines were a means of sorting out who belonged where. What was on your plate and in your cup helped to define your ethnicity, your class, your gender. In an age where most people existed on unexciting and rather lumpen fare – and where the daily menu was dictated by what could be grown and whatever the weather allowed – those with greater gastronomic choice had the luxury of using food as a statement.

At least some of those who shunned meat did so to set themselves apart from the carnivorous. Sometimes this was to voice religious dissent or, as in the case of Porphyry, to separate intellectuals and the philosophically enlightened from the unthinking masses. Jews used their dietary laws to avoid contamination and to separate themselves from the Gentiles. Thus, dietary restriction could act as a stratagem for thinking about awkward areas of identity. Eating different foods (or eating those foods in a different way) could act as points of certainty in a shifting ideological landscape. We have seen how the consumption of or abstention from fish (its actual practice and those texts that attempt to ideologically deconstruct fish-eating) could become a short-hand for concerns about social mobility and the potentially corrupting influences of wealth. We have also seen how fish occupied a number of positions along a spectrum of practices ranging from those who did not eat fish but venerated them (Syrians and Egyptians, or Roman aristocrats) to those who ate too many of them (greedy and corrupt Athenian politicians).

In the last chapter, I examined how some societies attempted to regulate the consumption of food and drink. It is, of course, a matter of speculation how far this was done for moral reasons and how far it was to do with the control of social mobility and political factions. However, it is important to remember that ancient authors very much emphasized the moral aspect. Excessive eating was seen as not only physically harmful, but morally wrong. Porphyry and Plutarch point to the way in which meat is deleterious to clear and effective thinking, whilst Cicero points a castigating finger at the intoxication of Mark Antony. Gluttony is often used as a symbol of internal corruption and moral failure (and by implication, abstinence is equated with virtue).

There are parallels with our own experience. Alarm at the rising level of obesity is often expressed in terms of its effect on mortality rates or national expenditure on health. However, it is also perceived as a moral issue. The adipose are stigmatized as lazy, lacking self-discipline. Fat is bad, but thin is morally pure: all hard work and denial. The thin person is conversant with the language of control: they suppress the impulse of hunger, they continue exercising when those around have collapsed in an heap. Thinness means power; the fat are weak. 'Control' is always found in the vocabulary of anorexics. Those who strive towards emaciation may do so for a number of reasons, but often take pride in assuming control of their bodies (when events in their lives are spiralling out of control). They talk of the discipline of self-denial; they see victory in every mouthful refused, defeat in each swallowed morsel.

Corpulence is the physical manifestation of an inner lack of restraint. In antiquity, the prime example of the man who lacks self-control was the tyrant, or absolute monarch. Adored and worshipped by an uncritical populace, freed from the fetters of law or conventional morality, he was at liberty to indulge every whim. He could circumvent or subvert traditional notions of what is appropriate and what is not. He could do things that may be considered unmanly: wear cosmetics or perfume, indulge in homosexual liaisons, with himself in the passive role. He might also eat to excess, as a display of ostentation and wealth, expressing the power to procure foods unavailable to the majority of his subjects.

This equation of overeating and tyrannical behaviour is common in Graeco-Roman texts. It is associated with the perceived decadence of the eastern world. As the Greeks and the Romans saw corruption and moral decay as emanating from the east (in terms of religion, custom and wealth), so the sensual, bloated and cruel monarch embodied all these vices. Tacitus rails in his *Annals* against

foreign customs that corrupt and degrade young Romans.[1] In his eyes, Nero, a
passionate devotee of Hellenic culture, is the embodiment of all that is wrong
with society, debauched, contaminated by foreign customs, increasingly effeminate, with a weak and corrupted aristocracy. Just as some today complain
of the decadence and immorality of youth, making nostalgic comparison
with their own thrift, order, and respect for authority, so ancient authors
distrusted what they saw as any subversion of hierarchy. This extends beyond
concern at social mobility to calling into question the very nature of identity
as notions of self capitulate before the blurring of traditional boundaries.

Gluttony, effeminacy and Eastern ethnicity (the last a category hard to
define and used by authors in a number of different ways) co-exist in classical
texts. If one extreme of ancient identity is the lean, spare warrior, content to
live a frugal existence, untainted and untempted by wealth or public acclaim,
but still of service to the state, at the other lies the spectre of the bloated, slug-
like male/female amalgam. This ambiguously gendered individual is cruel,
capricious, sensual and lives for the trappings of wealth, be they physical orna-
ment or luxurious banquets.

This image is often deployed to characterize the more problematic
emperors, particularly by Suetonius (writing in the second century AD, whose
biographies concern the emperors up to Domitian) and in the pages of the
*Scriptores Historia Augustae* (purporting to be have been composed by a
selection of authors writing during the reign of Diocletian at the end of the
third century AD, although more likely composed by a single hand at a much
later date). This second book contains putative biographies of emperors from
Hadrian onwards (biographies of Nerva and Trajan are lost to us). Much is of
dubious veracity and historians rely on the facts at their peril. Nevertheless,
they provide valuable information as to the way ancient moral character was
viewed. The fact that the character analysis of the *SHA* continues Suetonian
motifs points to the long-term validity of the stereotype of the voracious and
erratic monster that could be the absolute ruler.[2]

The twelfth book of Athenaeus is filled with examples of the archetypal
eastern tyrant. They mainly, though not exclusively, originated in Persia.[3] There

(1)       Tac. *Ann.* 14.15
(2)       For a stereotype is what it is, although of course it may provide a good indication as to
          the types of common prejudice that was current at the type (or a motif that may have
          reflected the ideologies or concerns of the text's potential readership).
(3)       Athenaeus asserts that Persians were the first race to become notorious for their devotion
          to pleasure; Ath. *Deip.* XII. 513e–f.

were also several Greek territories renowned for their devotion to luxury and epicurean living. The southern Italian city of Sybaris is a notable example (giving rise to sybarites), and Sicily, too, had the same reputation. Etruscans and Egyptians came in for much the same description. Their perceived vices were embodied by classical authors in the person of the absolute ruler. Here, indolence, effeminacy and gluttony were magnified, as was a preoccupation with novelty.[4] Setting aside perfumery and clothing and attending only to eating, Athenaeus' inventory of tyrants cited *On Heracleia* by Nymphis of Heracleia who described Dionysius, the tyrant of that city, as choked by the folds of flesh that were the consequence of his morbid obesity.[5] Athenaeus also quoted Agarthachides on Magas of Cyrene in the third century BC, who suffered similar corpulence and died because of it.[6] In Egypt, both Ptolemy VII and his son Alexander were of massive girth. Ptolemy earned himself the nickname Physcon (Fat Belly).[7] By contrast, Agarthachides noted that the virtuous Spartans (whose austerity we have already discussed) used to hold regular inspections of naked warriors to check that none had a protruding belly.[8]

The presumption of many philosophers and intellectuals was that preoccupation with food (certainly with meat) distracted from mental activities and contemplation of the divine. Pangs of hunger were a reminder of bodily demands, but could be resisted by the exercise of will. Hence greed implied no self-control. The ruler unable to resist physical desires was unable to make balanced moral judgements. As was noted in my opening chapter, both Claudius and Nero were judged poor rulers. They were self-indulgent, in thrall to slaves and women (in particular Nero's mother and Claudius' last wife Agrippina), sadistic and unworthy to exercise power. What is unclear is whether their gluttony and lack of control was the cause or symptom of their failings. Another emperor characterized by incompetence, cruelty and a vast appetite was Vitellius, who reigned for a few months in AD 69. Our principal source is Suetonius who described his eating habits as follows: 'He divided up his feasts into three or four parts: breakfast, lunch, dinner and a carousal. He was able to indulge in all this by using emetics.'[9] His claim to

(4)     Again, the Persians have a reputation as culinary innovators; Ath. *Deip*. XII. 515b–c. This linking of experimentation with food and tyranny is taken up again in the life of Elagabalus (also known as Heliogabalus) in the *SHA*.
(5)     Athen. *Deip*. XII. 549a–b.
(6)     Athen. *Deip*. XII. 550c.
(7)     Athen. *Deip*. XII. 550b.
(8)     Athen. *Deip*. XII. 550d.
(9)     Suet. *Vitell*. 13; for more on his gluttony, see Greenhalgh (1975), 114.

fame was his invention of a dish called 'the Shield of Minerva', named for
the enormous platter upon which it was served. It contained a miasma of
ingredients, sourced from all over the empire, including pike livers, peacock
and pheasant brains and flamingo tongues. It was cooked to celebrate his
arrival in Rome as emperor. It was said that two thousand fish and seven
thousand birds were served at this feast. [10]

An interesting fact about these three emperors is that their great appetites appeared unnatural. The word was that they relied on emetics to rid
themselves of food.[11] Nero may have done this for reasons of vanity and to
check his weight, but Claudius and Vitellius forcibly ejected food to make
room for more. The impetus was greed and it pushed the body beyond the
limits what was physically and, by implication, morally permissible. An
emperor is an exceptional individual and some separation from the ordinary
man was understood, but stuffing one's face until one vomits was not perhaps
the most desirable image (at least in the eyes of imperial biographers).

An example of such tensions is the boy-emperor Elagabalus.[12] This strange
figure represented all the ideals and attitudes that were the very opposite to
how Romans liked to view themselves. This teenager, master of much of the
known world, threatened to smash it apart. He was Syrian, the supposed son
of the emperor Caracalla, dominated by his mother Julia Soaemis and by his
grandmother Julia Maesa (sister of Julia Domna, the wife of Septimius Severus).
Elagabalus flaunted his bisexuality, he cross-dressed and indulged in extreme
forms of opulence. In addition, he advocated a form of (pagan) monotheism,
rejecting the Roman pantheon. Unmanly depravities, unacceptable behaviour
and his blurring and erosion of the limits of identity made him a fascinating
but ultimately perilous figure to the author(s) of the *SHA*. Dio told how this
refusal to accept a settled identity extended even to his gender:

> He brought his licentiousness to such a point that he asked his doctors
> to contrive a woman's vagina in his body, having offered them great
> sums to do this.[13]

(10)      Suet. *Vitell.* 13.2.
(11)      For Vitellius and emetics, see Suet. *Vitell.* 13.1; Dio *Epitome Bk LXIV* 2.2; (1975), 114;
          Crichton (1996), 203–207.
(12)      For Elagabalus, see Kettenhofen (1979); Frey (1989).
(13)      Cassius Dio LXXX. 16. 7.

The *Scriptores Historia Augustae* devoted disproportionate space to his banquets and culinary innovations. These included never serving seafood when dining near the coast, but only when far inland.[14] He also used to serve dishes fashioned out of wood or stone to the bemusement of his guests.[15] For him, meals were more than opportunities for nutrition, they were an arena for artistic statement, a display of largesse, chances to stage elaborate practical jokes. The *SHA*'s fascination was evidently down to curiosity, and might also demonstrate the centrality of food habits to the depiction of character. The book tapped into a cliché equating tyranny to corrupt eastern morals and overeating. Just as Augustus was good and therefore abstemious, and the philosophical equanimity of Marcus Aurelius was marked by lack of interest in fine food, so the despot was a wanton homosexual (who takes the passive role in intercourse), wilful, cowardly, drenched in perfume, addicted to luxury and an outrageous glutton. The connection between abstinence and virtue is taken up by the early Christians. Such a view was a reaction to the literary *topos*, if not the reality, of the profligate, fat pagan despot. This notion has a new currency today, superseding our earlier stereotype of the jolly giant.

(14)    SHA *Heliogab.* XXIII.8–XXIV.1.
(15)    SHA *Heliogab.* XXV.7–9.

# CONCLUSION

What should we make of dietary restriction in antiquity? It is evident there existed two almost separate worlds, of actual practice and of the realm of literature. They occasionally intersect, but generally run parallel to each other. While I have noted how religious or cultural norms dictated the types of food which were shunned, and how on occasion abstinence was required by custom or law, my chief interest has been how literary texts used dietary restriction as fact or metaphor. Some tried (or purported to try) to give a factual account and explain the reasons for this or that food habit or prejudice. However, often this was but the starting point. Authors used notions of excess or abstinence to explore ethnicity, religion and culture. Their opinions often reflected uncertainties and anxieties in a cultural landscape experiencing profound and violent change. We can discern profound misgivings about the level and speed of change, or attempts to assert and define ethnic identity. For example, the sumptuary laws of the late Roman republic were used by some authors, such as the elder Pliny and Aelian, to promote a conservative agenda, whereby conspicuous consumption is both a cause and a symptom of moral and political disintegration. These writers, profoundly uncomfortable with the changes wrought by relatively rapid political expansion, an influx of wealth, and population movements, urge an ideological shift and a return to an heroic uncorrupted past. Dietary simplicity is one facet of their nostalgia. During the Second Sophistic (that resurgence of Greek philosophy and intellectual life that dated from the reign of Nero and continued into the third century AD), Greek-speaking writers sought to reassert Greek identity under Roman rule by reconstructing it in the mould of the Homeric past. Just as Roman writers mythologized their own antecedents in search of a fixed identity, so too did Greeks. Athenaeus' dinner party existed in a bubble.[1] Its location may be Rome in the late second century AD, but its collective mind was far away celebrating and dissecting the literature and ideas of the diners' Greek heritage: a veritable orgy of cultural self-celebration and an act of voluntary cultural isolation.

Dietary self-abnegation is a vital element of this re-invention. The heroes of the past, be they paragons of Roman republican virtue or the Homeric warrior aristocracy, were partly defined by their simple diet. Excess food, or sophisticated foreign cuisines were metaphors (and hallmarks) of weakness and moral decay.[2] Moral and physical strength was founded upon dietary discipline. In a similar vein, philosophers and intellectuals from Plato onwards sought to foster the idea of a separation of mind and body whereby the physical was either irrelevant or detrimental to the spiritual. Food dulled the senses, and prevented mind's ascendancy. Porphyry exhorted the intelligentsia to embrace vegetarianism and reject the contaminating influences of the sensory world.

If it may be confidently asserted that dietary restriction could be an effective tool for self-identification, then it could also be used to define and classify others. Dietary laws ensured the preservation of Jewish identity in the Diaspora, and maintained ritual purity. However, Jewish diet could also be a way of defining them in the eyes of outsiders. Of the many special laws and customs adhered to by Jews, it is usually their diet – and *ad nauseam* their refusal to eat pork – that sets them apart in the eyes of Greek and Roman writers

While used to promote a conservative view of the world, diet and its manipulation was also a counter-cultural phenomenon, challenging orthodoxy. The Jews' pork taboo showed them unwilling to integrate with Graeco-Roman culture. Similarly, vegetarianism is tainted with a refusenik reputation, a rejection of conventional pieties and rituals, its unorthodox status reinforced by association with esoteric ideologies: the mysticism of Pythagoreans or the plea for compassion by Plutarch. This caused the majority to lump them in with Jewish ideology and Egyptian practices. The bean taboo, also associated

(1)     In spite of the presence of Larensis, the focus of the prandial conversation is the past. Braund argues otherwise; Braund (2000).

(2)     The oriental tyrants of Book XII of the *Deipnosophistae* are characterized by both excess and extravagance. The culinary oddities of Elagabalus act as a metaphor for his Syrian strangeness, his effeminacy and the alien nature of his religious practices; SHA *Heliogab*.

with the Pythagorean school, raises analogous concerns about the relationship between mainstream ideology and nonconformist behaviour.

This dichotomy between dietary restriction as a force both for conservatism and for unorthodoxy is but one problem we face when attempting to provide a coherent account. Classical authors (representing the moneyed élite, not the majority) may lead us to assume that food was a source of concern for those in authority and needed strict controls to regulate its use. This was true to a degree. The Roman sumptuary laws, and possibly archaic Spartan legislation, reflect an impetus towards moral control and an attempt to keep under control the spending habits (and the political ambitions) of the aristocracy. A restriction upon the amount that could be spent upon food, or the types of food that could be purchased, was regarded necessary to ensure there were sanctions to hand to enforce compliance. Writers might have urged self-discipline, but the existence of these laws (and in the case of the Roman sumptuary laws, legislation that was redrafted and reintroduced over many years) seems to indicate a reluctance on the part of many to heed their advice.

Self-regulation was apparently thought sufficient to control the use of alcohol. In spite of its great potential for misbehaviour and social disorder, evidence does not suggest rules existed to govern its sale and ingestion (even to or by the lower orders). The limits of drinking were often set by peer-pressure. Intoxication was regarded as something that should be policed by one's fellow drinkers, rather than by laws or governments.

For the majority of people, a restricted diet must have been omnipresent. For them, diet and identity was not an issue. The affluent, however, whose means transcended the view of food as fuel, saw it as a way of expressing identity, when lines marking the boundaries of religion, ethnicity and culture had become blurred, even dissolved. In a world where the terms Greek, Roman and barbarian had ceased to provide an effective means of identification, and when Roman citizenship was extended to millions of people, diet became another way of taking back local and individual identity. Its malleability meant that it could be used to both challenge the *status quo* and reinforce it.

# ABBREVIATIONS

| | |
|---|---|
| Ael. | Aelian |
| VH | Varia Historia |
| Apoll. Rhod. | Apollonius Rhodius |
| *Argon.* | *Argonautica* |
| App. | Appian |
| *Rom. Hist.* | *Roman History* |
| Apollod. | Apollodorus mythographus |
| *Bibl.* | *Bibliotheca* |
| Ar. | Aristophanes |
| *Av.* | *Aves* |
| *Thesm.* | *Thesmophoriazusae* |
| Arist. | Aristotle |
| *Hist. an.* | *Historia animalium* |
| *Pol.* | *Politica* |
| *Pr* | *Problemata* |
| *Rhet.* | *Rhetoric* |
| Arr. | Arrianus |
| *Epict. diss.* | *Epicteti dissertationes* |
| Ath. | Athenaeus |
| *Deip.* | *Deipnosophistae* |
| August. | Augustine |
| *De civ. D* | *De civitate Dei* |
| Cass. Dio | Cassius Dio |
| Cato | Cato Maior |
| *Agr.* | *De Agricultura or De Re Rustica* |
| Catull. | Catullus |
| *Carmin.* | *Carmina* |
| Cic. | Cicero (Marcus Tullius) |
| *Att.* | *Epistulae ad Atticum* |
| *Cael.* | *Pro Caelio* |
| *Div.* | *De divinatione* |
| *Leg.* | *De legibus* |
| *Phil.* | *Orationes Philippicae* |
| *Pis.* | *In Pisonem* |

Clem. Al.      Clemens Alexandrinus
   *Protr.*          *Protrepticus*
   *Protr. Beb.*      *To the Newly Baptized*
Columella
   *Rust.*          *De re rustica*
Deut.          Deuteronomy
Diod. Sic.     Diodorus Siculus
Diog. Laert.   Diogenes Laertius
   *Pythag.*        *Pythagoras*
Dioscor.       Dioscorides
   *De mat. med.*    *De materia medica*
Eur.           Euripides
   *Bacc.*          *Bacchae*
Euseb.         Eusebius
   *Hist. eccl.*      *Historia ecclesiastica*
FHG            Fragmenta Historicorum Graecorum
Gal.           Galen
   *De al. fac.*      *De alimentorum facultatibus*
   *QAM*            *quod animi mores corporis temperamentis sequantur*
Gell.          Aulus Gellius
   *NA*            *Noctes Atticae*
Hdt.           Herodotus
Hes.           Hesiod
   *Op.*           *Opera et Dies*
   *Sc.*           *Scutum*
   *Theog.*         *Theogonia*
Hippoc.        Hippocrates
   *De prisc. med.*   *De priscina medicina*
Hom.           Homer
   *Il.*            *Iliad*
   *Od.*           *Odyssey*
Hor.           Horace
   *Ars. P.*         *Ars poetica*
   *Carm.*          *Carmina*
   *Sat.*           *Satirae*
Iambl.         Iamblichus
   *VP*            *de vita Pythagorica*

| | |
|---|---|
| Joseph. | Josephus |
| *AJ* | *Antiquitates Judaicae* |
| *Ap.* | *Contra Apionem* |
| *Vit.* | *Vita* |
| Juv. | Juvenal |
| Levit. | Leviticus |
| LSJ | Liddell and Scott, *Greek-English Lexicon* |
| Lucian | Lucian |
| *Somn.* | *Somnium* |
| *Syr. D.* | *De Syria dea* |
| *Vit. auct.* | *Vitarum auctio* |
| Macrob. | Macrobius |
| *Sat.* | *Saturnalia* |
| Mart. | Martial |
| *Epig.* | *Epigrams* |
| Opp. | Oppian |
| *Halieut.* | *Halieutica* |
| Ov. | Ovid |
| *Fast.* | *Fasti* |
| *Met.* | *Metamorphoses* |
| Paus. | Pausanias |
| Philo | Philo Judaeus |
| *In Flacc.* | *In Flaccum* |
| *Leg.* | *Legatio ad Gaium* |
| Pind. | Pindar |
| *Ol.* | *Olympian Odes* |
| Pl. | Plato |
| *Leg.* | *Leges* |
| *Resp.* | *Respublica* |
| *Symp.* | *Symposium* |
| *Ti.* | *Timaeus* |
| Plaut. | Plautus |
| *Aul.* | *Aulularius* |
| Plin. | Pliny (the Elder) |
| *HN* | *Naturalis historia* |
| Plut. | Plutarch |
| *Alex.* | *Alexander* |

| | |
|---|---|
| Plut. | Plutarch (*contd.*) |
| *Brut.* | *Brutus* |
| *Cat. Mai.* | *Cato the Elder* |
| *Cic.* | *Cicero* |
| *De cap.* | *De capienda ex inimicis utilitate* |
| *De esu. carn.* | *De esu carnum* |
| *De Is. et Os.* | *De Iside et Oriside* |
| *De soll. an.* | *De sollertia animalium* |
| *De superst.* | *De superstition* |
| *Inst. Lac.* | *Instituta Laconica* |
| *Lucull.* | *Lucullus* |
| *Lyc.* | *Lycurgus* |
| *Quaest. Graec.* | *Quaestiones Graecae* |
| *Quaest. Rom.* | *Quaestiones Romanae* |
| *Quaest. conviv.* | *Quaestiones convivales* |
| *Sol.* | *Solon* |
| Polyb. | Polybius |
| Porph. | Porphyry |
| *Abst.* | *De Abstinentia* |
| *VP* | *Vita Pythagorae* |
| SHA | Scriptores Historia Augustae |
| *Aurel.* | *Aurelianus* |
| *Hadr.* | *Hadrianus* |
| *Heliogab.* | *Heliogabalus* |
| *Sev.* | *Severus* |
| *Verus* | *Lucius Verus* |
| Sen. | Seneca (the Younger) |
| *Ben.* | *De beneficiis* |
| *Ep.* | *Epistulae* |
| Sext. Emp. | Sextus Empiricus |
| *Pyr.* | *Outlines of Pyrrhonism* |
| Stob. | Stobaeus |
| *Flor.* | *Anthology* |
| Strabo | Strabo |
| *Geog.* | *Geographia* |
| Suet. | Suetonius |
| *Aug.* | *Divus Augustus* |

| | |
|---|---|
| Suet. | Suetonius (*contd.*) |
| *Calig.* | *Gaius Caligula* |
| *Claud.* | *Divus Claudius* |
| *Iul.* | *Divus Iulius* |
| *Ner.* | *Nero* |
| *Tib.* | *Tiberius* |
| Syll³ | Sylloge Inscriptionum Graecarum |
| Tac. | Tacitus |
| *Ann.* | *Annales* |
| Val. Max. | Valerius Maximus |
| Varro | Varro |
| *Rust.* | *De re rustica* |
| Vell. Pat. | Velleius Paterculus |
| Verg. | Virgil |
| *Aen.* | *Aeneid* |
| Vitr. | Vitruvius |
| *De arch.* | *De architectura* |
| Xen. | Xenophon |
| *An.* | *Anabasis* |
| *Lac.* | *Respublica Lacedaemoniorum* |
| *Mem.* | *Memorabilia* |

# BIBLIOGRAPHY

Africa, T.W. (1960) 'Phylarchus, Toynbee, and the Spartan Myth', 266–272, in *Journal of the History of Ideas*, Vol. 21, No. 2.

Alcock, J.P. (2001) *Food in Roman Britain*, Stroud.

Alston, R. (1997) 'Philo's "In Flaccum": Ethnicity and Social Space in Roman Alexandria', 165–175, in *Greece & Rome*, 2nd Ser., Vol. 44, No.2.

Andrews, A.C. (1949) 'The Bean and Indo-European Totemism', 274–292, in *American Anthropologist*, New Series, Vol. 51, No. 2.

–––– (1958) 'The Parsnip as a Food in the Classical Era', 145–152, in *Classical Philology*, Vol. 53, No. 3.

Angel, J.L. (1972) 'Ecology and Population in the Eastern Mediterranean', 88–105, in *World Archaeology*, Vol. 4, No. 1, Population.

Armstrong, A.H. (ed.) (1986) *Classical Mediterranean Spirituality: Egyptian, Greek, Roman*, New York.

Arnott, W.G., (1996) *Alexis: The Fragments. A Commentary*, Cambridge.

Astin, A.E. (1978) *Cato the Censor*, Oxford.

Athanassiadi, P. and Frede, M. (2001) *Pagan Monotheism in Late Antiquity*, Oxford.

Aubert, J-J., 'The Republican Economy and Roman Law: Regulation, Promotion or Reflection', 160–178, in Flower (2004).

Baldwin, B. (1995) 'Roman Emperors in the Elder Pliny', 56–78, in *Scholia,* Vol. 5.

Balme, M. (1984) 'Attitudes to Work and Leisure in Ancient Greece', 140–152, in *Greece & Rome,* 2nd Ser., Vol. 31, No. 2.

Barclay, J.M.G. (1996) *Jews in the Mediterranean Diaspora: From Alexander to Trajan (323 BCE–117 CE)*, Berkeley, CA.

Barr, A. (1998) *Drink: A Social History*, London.

Bazell, D.M. (1997) 'Strife among the Table-Fellows: Conflicting Attitudes of Early and Medieval Christians toward the Eating of Meat', 73–99, in *Journal of the American Academy of Religion*, Vol. 65, No. 1.

Baumgarten, A, 'Graeco-Roman Voluntary Associations and Ancient Jewish Sects', 93–110, in Goodman (ed.) (1973).

Beer, M. ""The question is not, Can they *reason*?, nor, Can they *talk*? But, Can they *suffer*?": The Ethics of Vegetarianism in the Writings of Plutarch', 96–109, in Grumett and Muers (2008).

Bekker-Nielsen, T. 'The Technology and Productivity of Ancient Sea Fishing',
    83–95, in Bekker-Nielsen (2005).
––––– (ed.) (2005) *Ancient Fishing and Fish Processing in the Black Sea Region*, Aarhus.
Belfiore, E. (1986) 'Wine and Catharsis of the Emotions in Plato's Laws', 421–437, in
    *The Classical Quarterly*, New Series, Vol. 36, No. 2.
Bell, H.L. (1941) 'Anti-Semitism in Alexandria', 1–18, in *The Journal of Roman
    Studies*, Vol. 31.
Bemporad, J.R. (1996) 'Self-starvation through the ages', 217–237, in *International
    Journal of Eating Disorders*, Vol. 19, No. 3.
Bendlin, A. 'Purity and Pollution', 178–189, in Ogden (2007).
Bengtson, H. (1968) *The Greeks and the Persians From the Sixth to the Fourth
    Centuries*, London.
Boardman, J. (1976) 'The Olive in the Mediterranean: Its Culture and Use', 187–194,
    in *Philosophical Transactions of the Royal Society of London*. Series B. Biological
    Sciences, Vol. 275, No. 936.
Bowersock, G.W. (1965) *Augustus and the Greek World*, Oxford.
––––– (ed.) (1973) *Approaches to the Second Sophistic*, University Park, PA.
Bowie, A.M. (1997) 'Thinking with Drinking: Wine and the Symposium in
    Aristophanes', 1–21, in *The Journal of Hellenic Studies*, Vol. 117.
Braudel, F. (1998) *The Mediterranean in the Ancient World*, London.
Braun, T. 'Barley Cakes and Emmer Bread', 25–37, in Wilkins *et al* (1995).
Braund, D. (1994) 'The Luxuries of Athenian Democracy', 41–48, in *Greece &
    Rome,* 2nd Ser., Vol. 41, No. 1.
––––– 'Learning, Luxury and Empire: Athenaeus' Roman Patron', 3–22, in Braund
    & Wilkins (2000).
Braund, D. & Wilkins, J. (eds) (2000) *Athenaeus and His World: Reading Greek
    Culture in the Roman Empire*, Exeter.
Bremner, J.N. (1992) 'Symbols of Marginality from early Pythagoreanism to Late
    Antique Monks', 205–214, in *Greece & Rome,* 2nd Ser. Vol. 39 No. 2.
––––– 'Greek Normative Animal Sacrifices', 132–144, in Ogden (2007).
Brock, R. and Wirtjes, H. 'Athenaeus on Greek Wine', 455–465, in Braund *et al*
    (2000).
Brothwell, P., Brothwell, D. (1998) *Food in Antiquity*, Baltimore, MD.
Brown, P. (1988) *The Body and Society: Men, Women and Sexual Renunciation in
    early Christianity*, Berkeley, CA.
Bruit, L. (1983) *Sacrifices non-sanglants et offrandes végétales en Grèce ancienne:
    rites et idéologies,* unpublished PhD thesis, l'Ecole pratique des Hautes Etudes
    (Sciences Réligieuses), Sorbonne.
Brumberg-Kraus, J. (1999) 'Meat-Eating and Jewish Identity: Ritualisation of
    the Priestly "Torah of Beast and Fowl" (Lev. 11:46) in Rabbinic Judaism and
    Medieval Kabbalah', 227–262, in *AJS Review*, Vol. 24, No. 2.
Brumfield, A.C. (1981) *The Attic Festivals of Demeter and their Relation to the
    Agricultural Year*, Salem, NH.
Bruun, C. (1997) 'Water for Roman Brothels: Cicero "Cael." 34', 364–373, in
    *Phoenix*, Vol.51, No. 3/4.

Burkert, W. (1972) *Lore and Science in Ancient Pythagoreanism*, trans. by Miner, E.L., Cambridge, MA.

———— (1983) *Homo Necans: The Anthropology of Ancient Greek Sacrificial Ritual and Myth*, trans. by Bing, P., Berkeley and Los Angeles.

———— (1985) *Greek Religion*, trans. by Raffan, J., Oxford.

———— (1987) *Ancient Mystery Cults*, Cambridge, MA.

Burris, E.E. (1929) 'The Nature of Taboo and Its Survival in Roman Life', 142–163, in *Classical Philology*, Vol. 24, No. 2.

Butrica, J.I.. (1999a) 'Using Water "Unchastely": Cicero "Pro Caelio" 34 Again', 136–139, in *Phoenix*, Vol. 53, No. 1/2.

———— (1999b) 'Using Water "Unchastely": Cicero "Pro Caelio" 34 Again-Addendum', 336, in *Phoenix*, Vol. 53, No. 3/4.

Cameron, A. (1991) 'How Thin was Philitas?' 534–538, in *The Classical Quarterly*, New Series, Vol. 41, No. 2.

Camporesi, P. (1998) *The Incorruptible Flesh: Bodily mutation and mortification in religion and folklore*, Cambridge.

Carlson, D.,W. (1998) '"Drinks He to His Own Undoing": Temperance Ideology in the Deep South', 659–691, in *Journal of the Early Republic*,Vol. 18, No. 4.

Cartledge, P. (1993) *The Greeks: A Portrait of Self and Others*, Oxford.

———— 'What have the Spartans done for us: Sparta's contribution to western civilisation', 164–179, in *Greece & Rome*, Oct 2004, Vol. 51, no. 2.

Cherry, D. (ed.) (2001) *The Roman World: A Source* Book, Oxford.

Churchill Semple, E. (1921) 'Geographic Factors in the Ancient Mediterranean Grain Trade', 47–74, in *Annals of the Association of American Geographers*, Vol. 11.

Clark, G. (trans.) (1989) *Iamblichus: On the Pythagorean way of life*, Liverpool.

———— (trans.) (2000) *Porphyry: On abstinence from killing animals*, London.

———— (2000) 'Animal Passions', 88–93, in *Greece & Rome*, 2nd Ser., Vol. 47, No. 1.

Cohen, S.J.D., Frerichs, E.S. (eds.) (1993) *Diasporas in Antiquity*, Atlanta, GA.

Cohen, S.J.D. (1999) *The Beginnings of Jewishness: Boundaries, Uncertainties, Varieties,* Berkeley, CA.

Collins, J.H. (1955) 'Some Roman Dinner Tables', 255–260,270, in *The Classical Journal*, Vol. 50, No. 6.

Combellack, F.M. (1953) 'Homer's Savage Fish', 257–261, in *The Classical Journal*, Vol. 48, No. 7.

Commager, S. (1957) 'The Function of Wine in Horace's Odes', 68–80, in *Transactions and Proceedings of the American Philological Association*, Vol. 88.

Cook, J.M. (1962) *The Greeks in Ionia and the East*, London.

Corcoran, T.H. (1963) 'Roman Fish Sauces', 204–210, in *The Classical Journal*, Vol. 58, No. 5.

———— (1964) 'Fish Treatises in the Early Roman Empire', 271–274, in *The Classical Journal*, Vol. 59, No. 6.

Costa, C.D. (ed.) (1974) *Seneca*, London.

Couch, H.N. (1936) 'Fishing in Homer', 303–314, in *The Classical Journal*, Vol. 31, No. 5.

Coveney, J. (2001) *Food, morals, and meaning: the pleasure and anxiety of eating*, London.

Craik, E. 'Diet, *diaita* and dietetics', 387–402, in Powell (1995).

Crawford, D.J. (1979) 'Food: Tradition and Change in Hellenistic Egypt', 136–146, in *World Archaeology*, Vol. 11, No. 2, Food and Nutrition.

Crawford, M. (1992) *The Roman Republic*, 2nd edition, London.

Crichton, P. (1996) 'Were the Roman Emperors Claudius and Vitellius bulimic?' 203–207, in *International Journal of Eating Disorders*, Vol. 19, No. 2.

Crook, J.A., Lintott, A., Rawson, E. (eds.) (1994) *The Cambridge Ancient History Volume IX: The Last Age of the Roman Republic, 146–43 BC*, Second Edition, Cambridge.

Cubberley, A. 'Bread-baking in Ancient Italy: *clibanus* and *sub testu* in the Roman World', 55–68, in Wilkins *et al* (1995).

Culham, P. 'Women in the Roman Republic', 139–159, in Flower (2004).

Cumont, F. (1956) *Oriental Religions in Roman Paganism*, New York.

Curtis, R.I. (2001) *Ancient Food Technology*, Leiden, Boston, Köln.

– – – – 'Sources for the Production and Trade of Greek and Roman Processed Fish', 31–46, in Bekker-Nielsen (2005).

Dalby, A. (1995) *Siren Feasts: a history of food and gastronomy in Greece*, London.

– – – – (2000) *Empire of pleasures: luxury and indulgence in the Roman world*, London.

– – – – (2003) *Food in the Ancient World*, London & New York.

Daniel, J.L. (1979) 'Anti-Semitism in the Hellenistic-Roman Period', 45–65, in *Journal of Biblical Literature*, Vol. 98, No. 1.

D'Arms, J.H. 'Heavy Drinking and Drunkenness in the Roman World: Four Questions for Historians', 304–317, in Murray and Tecusan (1995).

David, E. (1978) 'The Spartan Syssitia and Plato's Laws', 486–495, in *The American Journal of Philology*, Vol. 99, No. 4.

Davidson, J. (1993) 'Fish, Sex and Revolution in Athens', 53–66, in *The Classical Quarterly*, Vol. 43, No. 1.

– – – – 'Opsophagia: Revolutionary Eating at Athens', 204–213, in Wilkins *et al* (1995).

– – – – 'On the fish missing from Homer', 57–64, in Wilkins (1996).

– – – – (1997a) 'A Ban on Public Bars in Thasos?' 392–395, in *The Classical Quarterly*, New Series, Vol.47, No. 2.

– – – – (1997b) *Courtesans and Fishcakes*, London.

Davis, R. (1971) 'The Roman Military Diet', 122–142, in *Britannia*, Vol. 2.

Delwiche, C.C. (1978) 'Legumes-Past, Present, and Future', 565–570, in *BioScience*, Vol. 28, No.9.

Dench, E. 'Austerity, Excess, Success, and Failure in Hellenistic and Early Imperial Italy', 121–146, in Wyke (1998a).

Detienne, M. (1977) *Gardens of Adonis: Spices in Greek Mythology*, trans. by Lloyd, J., Princeton, NJ.

Detienne, M. & Vernant, J-P. (1989) *The Cuisine of Sacrifice among the Greeks*, translated by Wissing, P., Chicago and London.

De Vogel, C.J. (1966) *Pythagoras and Early Pythagoreanism*, Utrecht.

Diller, A. (1937) *Race Mixture among the Greeks before Alexander*, Westport, CT.

Dillon, J. & Herschbell, J. (trans.)(1991) *Iamblichus: On the Pythagorean Way of Life*, Atlanta.

Dillon, M. (2002) *Girls and Women in Classical Greek Religion*, London and New York.

Dittenberger, W. (1982) *Sylloge Inscriptionum Graecarum: Volumen Tertium*, Hidesheim, Zürich, New York.

Dodds, E.R. (1933) 'The Portrait of a Greek Gentleman', 97–107, in *Greece & Rome*, Vol. 2, No. 5.

Dombrowski, D. (1984a) *The Philosophy of Vegetarianism*, Amherst, MA.

———— (1984b) 'Vegetarianism and the Argument from Marginal Cases in Porphyry', 141–143, in *Journal of the History of Ideas*, Volume 45, No. 1.

Donfried, K.P., Richardson, P. (eds.)(1998) *Judaism and Christianity in First-Century Rome*, Cambridge.

Douglas, M.(1966) *Purity and Danger: An analysis of concepts of pollution and taboo*, London, Boston and Henley.

———— (ed.)(1984) *Food in the Social Order: Studies of Food and Festivities in Three American Communities*, New York.

———— (ed.)(1987) *Constructive Drinking: Perspectives on Drink from Anthropology*, Cambridge.

Dover, K.J. (1978) *Greek Homosexuality*, London.

Dudley, D.R. (1937) *A History of Cynicism*, London.

Dunbabin, K.M.D.(2003) *The Roman Banquet: Images of Conviviality*, Cambridge.

Dupont, F. (1992) *Daily Life in Ancient Rome*, trans. by Woodall, C., Oxford.

Easterling, P.E., Muir, J.V. (ed.) (1985) *Greek Religion and Society*, Cambridge. .

Edwards, C. (1993) *The Politics of Immorality in Ancient Rome*, Cambridge.

Ehrenberg, V. (1973) *From Solon to Socrates: Greek History and Civilisation during the sixth and fifth centuries B.C.*, second edition, London.

Elworthy, F.T. (1903) 'A Solution of the Gorgon Myth', 212–242, in *Folklore*, Vol. 14, No. 3.

Engels, D. (1978) 'A Note on Alexander's Death', 224–228, in *Classical Philology*, Vol. 73, No. 3.

Engs, R.C. (1995) 'Do Traditional Western European Drinking Practices have Origins in Antiquity?', 227–239, in *Addiction Research* 2(3).

Erdkamp, P.(1998) *Hunger and the Sword: Warfare and Food Supply in Roman Republican Wars (264–30 BC)*, Amsterdam.

Evans, H.B. (1997) *Water Distribution in Ancient Roman: The Evidence of Frontinus*, Ann Arbor, MI.

Evans, J.K.(1981) 'Wheat production and Its Social Consequences in the Roman World', 428–442, in *The Classical Quarterly*, New Series, Vol.31, No. 2.

Eyben, E. (1993) *Restless Youth in Ancient Rome*, London and New York.

Faas, P. (1994) *Around the Roman Table: Food and Feasting in Ancient Rome*, Chicago.

Farb, P., Armelagos, G. (1980) *Consuming Passions: the anthropology of eating*, New York.

Feeley-Harnik, G. (1981) *The Lord's Table: The Meaning of Food in Early Judaism and Christianity*, Washington.

–––– (1995) 'Religion and Food: An Anthropological Perspective', 565–582, in *Journal of the American Academy of Religion*, Vol. 63, No. 3.

Feldman, L.H., Hata, G. (1987) *Josephus, Judaism and Christianity*, Detroit, MI.

Feldman, L.H. (1988) 'Pro-Jewish Intimations in Anti-Jewish Remarks Cited in Josephus' "Against Apion"', 187–251, in *The Jewish Quarterly Review*, New Ser., Vol. 78, No. 3 / 4.

–––– (1993) *Jew and Gentile in the Ancient World: Attitudes and Interactions from Alexander to Justinian*, Princeton, NJ.

Ferguson, J. (1970) *The Religions of the Roman Empire*, London.

–––– (1980) *Greek and Roman Religion*, Park Ridge, NJ.

Ferguson, W.S. (1911) *Hellenistic Athens*, London.

Figueira, T.J. (1984) 'Mess Contributions and Subsistence at Sparta', 87–109, in *Transactions of the American Philological Association (1974–)*, Vol. 114.

Finley, M.I. (1973) *The Ancient Economy*, London.

Fisher, N.R.E. 'Drink, *Hybris* and the Promotion of Harmony in Sparta', 26–50, in Powell (1988).

Fisher, N. 'Symposiasts, Fish-Eaters and Flatterers: Social Mobility and Moral Concerns in Old Comedy', 355–396, in Harvey and Wilkins (2000).

Flint-Hamilton, K.B. (1999) 'Legumes in Ancient Greece and Rome: Food, Medicine, or Poison?' 371–385, in *Hesperia*, Vol. 68, No. 3.

Flower, H.I. (ed.)(2004) *The Cambridge Companion to the Roman Republic*, Cambridge.

Forbes, C.A. (1951) 'Beer: A Sober Account', 281–285,300, in *The Classical Journal*, Vol. 46, No. 6.

Forrest, W.G. (1963) 'The Date of the Lykourgan Reforms in Sparta', 157–179, in *Phoenix*, Vol.17, No.3.

Foxhall, L., Forbes, H.A. (1982) '*Sitometreia*: the role of grain as a staple food in classical antiquity', 41–90, in *Chiron* Band 12, Munich.

Frayn, J.M. (1974) 'Subsistence Farming in Italy during the Roman Period: A Preliminary Discussion of the Evidence', 11–18, in *Greece & Rome*, 2nd Ser., Vol. 21, No. 1.

–––– (1975) 'Wild and Cultivated Plants: A Note on the Peasant Economy of Roman Italy', 32–39, in *The Journal of Roman Studies*, Vol. 65.

Fraser, A.D. (1923) 'The Homeric Fish-Question', 240–242, in *The Classical Journal*, Vol. 18, No. 4.

Frey, M. (1989) *Untersuchungen zur Religion und zur Religionspolitik des Kaisers Elagabal*, Stuttgart.

Frey, R. (1983) *Rights, Killing and Suffering: Moral Vegetarianism and Applied Ethics*, Oxford.

Frost, F.J. (1968) 'Diving in Antiquity', 180–185, in *Greece & Rome*, Vol. 15, No.2.

Frost, S.W. (1934) 'Ancient Fish Admirers', 574–78, in *The Scientific Monthly*, Vol. 38, No. 6.

Gallant, T.W. (1985) *A Fisherman's Tale*, Ghent.

Gallant. T.W. (1991) *Risk and Survival in Ancient Greece: Reconstructing the Rural Domestic Economy*, Stanford.

Garnsey, P. (1988) *Famine and Food Supply in the Graeco-Roman World: Responses to Risk and Crisis*, Cambridge.

–––– (1998) *Cities, Peasants and Food in Classical Antiquity*, Cambridge.

–––– (1999) *Food and Society in Classical Antiquity*, Cambridge.

Gaskin, J. (ed.) (1995) *The Epicurean Philosophers*, London.

Gilhus, I.S. (2006) *Animals, Gods and Humans: Changing Attitudes to Animals in Greek, Roman and early Christian Ideas*, Oxford.

Gilliver, C.M. (1999) *The Roman Art of War*, Stroud.

Goldhill, S. (ed.) (2001) *Being Greek under Rome: Cultural Identity, the Second Sophistic and the Development of Empire*, Cambridge.

–––– (2004) *Love, Sex and Tragedy. How the Ancient World Shaped Our Lives*, London.

Goldstein, N.W. (1939) 'Cultivated Pagans and Ancient Anti-Semitism', 346–364, in *The Journal of Religion*, Vol. 19, No. 4.

Goodenough, E.R. (1962) *An Introduction to Philo Judaeus*, London.

Goodman, J., Lovejoy, P.E. and Sherratt, A. (eds.) (1995) *Consuming Habits: Drugs in History and Anthropology*, London and New York.

Goodman, M. (ed.) (1973) *Jews in a Graeco-Roman World*, Oxford.

–––– (1989) 'Nerva, the *Fiscus Judaicus* and Jewish Identity', 40–44, in *The Journal of Roman Studies*, Vol. 79.

–––– (1997) *The Roman World 44 BC–180 AD*, London.

Goody, J. (1982) *Cooking, Cuisine and Class: A Study in Comparative Sociology*, Cambridge.

Gorman, P. (1979) *Pythagoras: A Life*, London.

Gould, J. 'On making sense of Greek religion', 1–33, in Easterling and Muir (1985).

Gow, A.S.F. (1968) 'On the Haelieutica of Oppian', 60–8, in *The Classical Quarterly*, Vol. 18, No. 1.

Gowers, E. (1993) *The Loaded Table*, Oxford.

Grant, M. (1967), *Gladiators*, London.

–––– (1973) *The Jews in the Roman World*, London.

–––– (1995) *The Twelve Caesars*, London.

Grant, R.M. (1980) 'Dietary Laws among Pythagoreans, Jews, and Christians', 299–310, in *The Harvard Theological Review*, Vol. 73, No. 1–2.

Green, P. (1979) 'Ars Gratia Cultus: Ovid as Beautician', 381–392, in *The American Journal of Philology*, Vol. 100, No. 3.

–––– (1990) *Alexander to Actium: The Historical Evolution of the Hellenistic Age*, Los Angeles, CA.

Greenhalgh, P.A.L. (1975) *The Year of the Four Emperors*, London.

Grimm, V. 'Fasting Women in Judaism and Christianity in Late Antiquity', 225–240, in Wilkins *et al* (1995).

–––– (1996) *From Feasting to Fasting, and the evolution of a sin: Attitudes to Food in Late Antiquity*, London.

–––– (1999) 'On the Dietary habits of the Roman Empire as seen by outsiders, Jews and Christians', in *Classics Ireland* Vol.6. [electronic version: http://www.ucd. ie/classics/classicsinfo/99/grimm.html].

Grmek, M.D. (1983) *Diseases in the Ancient Greek World*, Baltimore and London.

Gruen. E.S. (1993) *Culture and National Identity in Republican Rome*, London.

———— (2002) *Diaspora: Jews amidst Greeks and Romans*, Cambridge, MA.

Grumett, D., Muers, R. (eds.)(2008) *Eating and Believing: Interdisciplinary Perspectives on Vegetarianism and Theology*, London.

Gusfield, J. 'Passage to play: rituals of drinking time in American society', 73–90, in Douglas (1987).

Hall, E. (1989) *Inventing the Barbarian: Greek Self-Definition through Tragedy*, Oxford.

Hall, J. (1997) *Ethnic Identity in Greek antiquity*, Cambridge.

Halstead, P. (1987) 'Traditional and Ancient Rural Economy in Mediterranean Europe: Plus ça Change?' 77–87, in *The Journal of Hellenic Studies*, Vol. 107.

Hammond, N.G.L. (1950) 'The Lycurgean Reform at Sparta', 42–64, in *The Journal of Hellenic Studies*, Vol.70.

Hardie, P. (1995) 'The Speech of Pythagoras in Ovid *Metamorphoses* 15: Empedoclean Epos', 204–214, in *The Classical Quarterly*, Volume 45, No. 1.

Harris, W.V., Ruffini, G. (eds.) (2004) *Ancient Alexandria between Egypt and Greece*, Leiden and Boston, MA.

Harrison, J.E. (1922) *Prolegomena to the Study of Greek Religion*, Cambridge.

Hartog, F. (1988) *The Mirror of Herodotus: The Representation of the Other in the Writing of History*, trans. by Lloyd, J., Berkeley, Los Angeles, London.

Harvey, D. and Wilkins, J. (eds.) (2000) *The Rivals of Aristophanes*, Swansea.

Head, B.V. (1911) *Historia Numorum: A Manual of Greek Numismatics*, Oxford.

Heath, M. 'Do Heroes Eat Fish? Athenaeus on the Homeric Lifestyle', 342–352, in Braund *et al* (2000).

Helmbold, W.C. (1950) 'The Complexion of Domitian', 388–389, in *The Classical Journal*, Vol. 45, No.8.

Henrichs, A. (1983) 'The "Sobriety" of Oedipus: Sophocles oc 100 Misunderstood', 87–100, in *Harvard Studies in Classical Philology*, Vol. 87.

Hewig, A. (1991) 'Ariadne's Fears from Sea and Sky (Ovid, Herioides 10.88 and 95–8)', 554–556, in *The Classical Quarterly*, Vol. 41, No 2.

Hirsch, S.W. (1986) 'Cyrus' Parable of the Fish: Sea Power in the Early Relations of Greece and Persia', 222–229, in *The Classical Journal*, Vol. 81, No. 3.

Hodkinson, S. (1983) *Social order and the conflict of values in classical Sparta*, Munich.

———— (2000) *Property and wealth in classical Sparta*, London.

Hodnett, M.P. (1919) 'The Sea in Roman Poetry', 67–82, in *The Classical Journal*, Vol. 15, No. 2.

Holladay, A.J. (1977) 'Spartan Austerity', 111–126, in *The Classical Quarterly*, New Series, Vol. 27, No. 1.

van Hoofe, A.J.L. (1990) *From Autothanasia to Suicide: Self-killing in Classical Antiquity*, London and New York. .

Hooke, S.H. (1961) 'Fish Symbolism', 535–538, in *Folklore*, Vol. 72, No. 3.

Hope, V.M., Marshall, E. (2000) *Death and Disease in the Ancient City*, London.

Hopkins, K. (1965) 'Elite Mobility in the Roman Empire', 12–26, in *Past and Present*, No. 32.

–––– (1999) *A World Full of Gods: Pagans, Jews and Christians in the Roman Empire*, London.

Horden, P., Purcell, N. (2000) *The Corrupting Sea. A Study of Mediterranean History*, Oxford.

Hornblower, S., Spawforth, A. (1996) *The Oxford Classical Dictionary (Third Edition)*, Oxford.

Huskinson, J. (ed.) (2000) *Experiencing Rome: Culture, Identity and Power in the Roman Empire*, Milton Keynes.

Hunt, A. (1996) *Governance of the Consuming Passions: A History of Sumptuary Law*, London.

Huxley, H.H. (1952) 'Storm and Shipwreck in Roman Literature', 117–124, in *Greece & Rome*, Vol. 21, No. 63.

Hyamson, M. (1897) 'Another Word on the Dietary Laws', 294–310, in *The Jewish Quarterly Review*, Vol. 9, No. 2.

Inwood, B. (2003) *The Cambridge Companion to the Stoics*, Cambridge.

Isaac, B. (2004) *The invention of racism in classical antiquity*, Princeton, NJ. and Oxford.

Jackson, R. (1988) *Doctors and Diseases in the Roman Empire*, London.

Jacobs, L. (1995) *The Jewish Religion*, Oxford.

Jacobsen, A.L.L. 'The Reliability of Fishing Statistics as a Source for Catches and Fish Stocks in Antiquity', 97–104, in Bekker-Nielsen (2005).

James, E.O. (1958) *Myth and Ritual in the Ancient Near East*, London.

Jasny, N. (1942) 'Competition Among Grains in Classical Antiquity', 747–764, in *The American Historical Review*, Vol. 47, No. 4.

–––– (1950) *The Daily Bread of the Ancient Greeks and Romans*, 227–253, in *Osiris*, Vol. 9.

Jenkins, G.K. (1972) *Ancient Greek Coins*, London.

Jouanna, J. and Villard, L. (eds.) (2002) *Vin et Santé en Grèce Ancienne*, Paris.

Kassel, R. and Austin, C. (eds.)(1983) *Poetae Comici Graeci*, Berlin and New York.

Kettenhofen, E. 'Die Syrische Augustae in der historische Überlieferung: ein Beitrag zum Problem der Oriëntalisierung',333, in *Antiquitas*. Reihe 3, bd. 24, 1979.

Kingsley, P. (1995) *Ancient Philosophy, Mystery, and Magic: Empedocles and Pythagorean Tradition*, Oxford.

Knox, P.E. (1985) 'Wine, Water, and Callimachean Polemics', 107–199, in *Harvard Studies in Classical Philology*, Vol. 89.

Kraemer, R.S. (1989) 'On the Meaning of the Term "Jew" in Graeco-Roman Inscriptions', 35–53, in *The Harvard Theological Review*, Vol. 82, No. 1.

Kuttner, A.L. 'Roman Art during the Republic', 294–321, in Flower (2004).

Kyle, D.G. (1998) *Spectacles of Death in Ancient Rome*, London.

Lawler, L.B. (1941) 'ΙΧΘΥΕΣ ΞΟΡΕΥΤΑΙ', 142–155, in *Classical Philology*, Vol. 36, No. 2.

Lawson, J. (1950) 'The Roman Garden', 97–105, in *Greece & Rome*, Vol. 19 No. 57.

Leary, T.J. (1993) 'Of Paul and Pork and Proselytes', 292–293, in *Novum Testamentum*, Vol. 35, Fasc. 3.

Leemon, T.A. (1972) *The Rites of Passage in a Student Culture: A Study of the Dynamics of Transition*, New York and London.

Lefkowitz, M.R. and Fant, M.B. (eds.)(2005) *Women's Life in Greece and Rome*, Third Edition, London.

Levick, B. (1982) 'Morals, Politics and the Fall of the Roman Republic', 53–62, in *Greece & Rome*, 2nd Ser, Vol. 29, No. 1.

Lèvy, I. (1927) *La légende de Pythagore de Grèce en Palestine*, Paris.

Lewis, N., Reinhold, M. (1990) *Roman Civilisation: Volume I: The Republic and the Augustan Age*, New York.

–––– (1990) *Roman Civilisation: Volume II: The Empire*, New York.

Lieu, J., North, J., Rajak, T. (eds.) (1992) *The Jews Among Pagans and Christians in the Roman Empire*, London and New York.

Lightfoot, J. L. (trans.)(2003) *Lucian: On the Syrian Goddess*, Oxford.

Linderski, J. (2001) ' "Imago Hortorum" : Pliny the Elder and the Gardens of the Urban Poor', 305–308, in *Classical Philology* Vol. 96 No. 3.

Lissarrague, F. (1990) *The Aesthetics of the Greek Banquet: Images of Wine and Ritual (Un Flot d'Images)*, Princeton, NJ.

Lobban Jr., R. A. (1994) 'Pigs and their Prohibition', 57–75, in *International Journal of Middle East Studies*, Vol. 26, No. 1.

Lomas, K. (1993) *Rome and the Western Greeks 350 BC–AD 200*, London and New York.

Lonsdale, S. H. (1979) 'Attitudes towards Animals in Ancient Greece', 146–159, in *Greece & Rome*, Volume 26, No. 2.

Lowrance, W.D. (1939) 'Roman Dinners and Diners', 86–91, in *The Classical Journal*, Vol. 35, No. 2.

Maas, M. (2000) *Readings in Late Antiquity: A Sourcebook*, London.

MacDowell, D. M. (1986) *Spartan Law*, Edinburgh.

MacMullen, R. (1981) *Paganism in the Roman Empire*, New Haven and London.

–––– (1996) *Enemies of the Roman Order: Treason, Unrest and Alienation in the Empire*, New York.

MacUrdy, G.H. (1930) 'The Refusal of Callisthenes to Drink the Health of Alexander', 294–297, in *The Journal of Hellenic Studies*, Vol.50, Part 2.

Manchester, K. (1984) 'Tuberculosis and Leprosy in Antiquity: An Interpretation', 162–173, in *Medical History*, 28.

Mandelbaum, D.G. (1965) 'Alcohol and Culture', 281–288, 289–293, in *Current Anthropology*, Vol. 6, No. 3.

March, J, (1998) *Dictionary of Classical Mythology*, London.

Mars, G. 'Longshore drinking, economic security and union politics in Newfoundland', 91–101, in Douglas, M.(1987).

Mars, G. & Mars, V. (1993) *Food, Culture and History* Vol. 1, The London Food Seminar.

Matthews, W. (1898) 'Icthyophobia', 105–112, in *The Journal of American Folklore*, Vol. 11, No. 41.

McKinlay, A.P. (1939) 'The "Indulgent" Dionysius, 51–61, in *Transactions and Proceedings of the American Philological Association*, Vol. 70.

──── (1946) 'The Wine Element in Horace', 161–167, in *The Classical Journal*, Vol. 42, No.3.

Meijer, F. (1986) *A History of Seafaring in the Classical World*, London and Sydney.

Mellor, R. (1993) *Tacitus*.

Merrill, E.T. (1919) 'The Expulsion of Jews from Rome under Tiberius', 365–372, in *Classical Philology*, Vol. 14, No. 4.

Michael, J.H. (1924) 'The Jewish Sabbath in the Latin Classical Writers', 117–124, in *The American Journal of Semitic Languages and Literatures*, Vol. 40, No. 2.

Michell, H. (1947) 'The Iron Money of Sparta', 42–44, in *Phoenix*, Vol. 1.

──── (1952) *Sparta*, Cambridge.

Mitchell, L. (forthcoming) *Panhellenism and the barbarian in archaic and classical Greece*, Swansea.

Miles, R. (1999) *Constructing Identities in Late Antiquity*, London and New York.

Millar, F. (1993) *The Roman Near East 31 BC–AD 337*, Cambridge, MA.

Modrzejewski, J.M. (1995) *The Jews of Egypt: From Rameses II to Emperor Hadrian*, Princeton, NJ.

Mills, H. (1984) 'Greek Clothing Regulations: Sacred and Profane', 255–265, in *Zeitschrift für Papyrologie und Epigraphik*, 55.

Momigliano, A. (1987) *On Pagans, Jews and Christians*, Middletown, CT.

Montefiore, C.G. (1896) 'Dr Wiener on the Dietary Laws', 392–413, in *The Jewish Quarterly Review*, Vol. 8, No. 3.

Montserrat, M., 'Reading gender in the Roman world', 153–181, in Huskinson (2000).

Moritz, L.A.(1955a) 'Corn', 135–141, in *The Classical Quarterly*, New Series, Vol. 5, No.3 / 4, 135–141.

──── (1955b) ' 'Husked' and 'Naked' Grain', 129–134, in *The Classical Quarterly*, New Series, Vol. 5, No3–4.

──── (1958) *Grain Mills and Flour in Classical Antiquity*, Oxford.

Morrison, J.S. (1956) 'Pythagoras of Samos', 135–156, in *The Classical Quarterly*, Vol.6, No. 314.

Mossman, J. (ed.)(1997) *Plutarch and His Intellectual World*, London.

Murray, O. (ed.)(1990) *Sympotica: A Symposium on the Symposion*, Oxford.

──── 'War and the Symposium', 83–104, in Slater (1991).

Murray, O. & Tecusan, M.(eds.)(1995) *In Vino Veritas*, London.

Mylona, D. (2008) *Fish Eating in Greece from the Fifth Century B.C. to the Seventh Century A.D. A story of impoverished fishermen or luxurious fish banquets?*, Oxford.

Myres, J.L.(1953) 'Ancient Groceries', 1–10, in *Greece & Rome*, Vol. 22, No. 64.

Neusner, J. (1975) 'The Idea of Purity in Ancient Judaism',15–26, in *Journal of the American Academy of Religion*, Vol.43, No.1.

Nisbet, G. (2003) 'A Sickness of Discourse: the Vanishing Syndrome of *Leptosune*', 191–205, in *Greece & Rome*, Vol. 50, No. 2.

North, J. (2000) *Greece & Rome: New Surveys in the Classics: No. 30: Roman Religion*, Oxford.

Noy, D. (2000) *Foreigners at Rome: Citizens and Strangers*, London.

Nutton, V.(1995) 'Galen and the Traveller's Fare', 359–370, in Wilkins *et al*(1995).

Ogden, D. (ed.) (2007) *Companion to Greek Religion*, Oxford.

Olson, S. D. and Sens, A. (trans.) (2000) *Archestratus of Gela: Greek Culture and Cuisine in the Fourth Century BCE*, Oxford.

Osborne, C. 'Ancient Vegetarianism', 214–223, in Wilkins *et al* (1995).

———— (2007) *Dumb Beasts and Dead Philosophers: Humanity and the Humane in Ancient Philosophy and Literature*, Oxford.

Ostenfeld, E.N. (ed.)(2001) *Greek Romans and Roman Greeks: Studies in Cultural Interaction*, Aarhus.

Otzen, B. (1990) *Judaism in Antiquity: Political Development and Religious Currents from Alexander to Hadrian*, Sheffield.

Parker, R. (1983) *Miasma: Pollution and Purification in early Greek Religion*, Oxford.

———— (1991) ' 'The Hymn to Demeter' and the 'Homeric Hymns'', 1–17, in *Greece & Rome*, 2nd Ser., Vol. 38, No. 1.

———— (2005) *Polytheism and Society at Athens*, Oxford.

Patterson, J.R. 'The City of Rome', 345–364, in Rosenstein and Morstein-Marx (2006).

Pettazzoni, R. (1937) 'Confession of Sins and the Classics', 1–14, in *The Harvard Theological Review*, Vol. 30, No. 1.

Pellizer, E. 'Outlines of a Morphology of Sympotic Entertainment', 177–183, in Murray (1990).

Philip, J.A. (1959) 'The Biographical Tradition-Pythagoras', 185–194, in *Transactions and Proceedings of the American Philological Association*, Vol. 90.

———— (1963a) 'Aristotle's Sources for Pythagorean Doctrine', 251–265, in *Phoenix*, Vol. 17, 4.

———— (1963b) 'Aristotle's Monograph *On the Pythagoreans*', 185–198, in *Transactions and Proceedings of the American Philological Association*, Vol. 94.

———— (1966) *Pythagoras and Early Pythagoreanism*, Toronto.

Phillips, J.W. and Staley, H.K.(1961) 'Sumptuary Legislation in Four Centuries', 673–677, in *Journal of Home Economics*, Vol. 53, No. 8.

Plass, P. (1995) *The Game of Death in Ancient Rome: Arena Sport and Political Suicide*, Madison, WI.

Poggie, J.J., Gersuny, C. (1972) 'Risk and Ritual: An Interpretation of Fishermen's Folklore in a New England Community', 66–72, in *The Journal of American Folklore*, Vol. 85, No. 335.

Poggie, J.J., Pollnac, R.B (1976) 'Risk as a Basis for Taboos among Fishermen in Southern New England', 257–262, in *Journal for the Scientific Study of Religion*, Vol. 15, No. 3.

Pomeroy, S.B. (1975) *Goddesses, Whores, Wives, & Slaves*, London.

Powell, A. (ed.)(1988) *Classical Sparta: techniques behind her success*, Oklahoma.

———— (ed.)(1995) *The Greek World*, London.

Preston, R., 'Roman questions, Greek answers: Plutarch and the construction of identity', 86–119, in Goldhill (2001).

Purcell, N. (1985) 'Wine and Wealth in Ancient Italy', 1–19, in *The Journal of Roman Studies*, Vol. 75.

Purcell, N. 'Eating Fish: The Paradoxes of Seafood', 132–149, in Wilkins *et al* (1995).

–––– (2003) 'The Way We Used to Eat: Diet, Community and History at Rome', 329–358, in *American Journal of Philology*, Volume 124, No. 3.

Pütz, B. (2007) *Symposium and Komos in Aristophanes*, Stuttgart and Weimar.

Radin, M. (1922) 'Homer and Little Fishes', 461–463, in *The Classical Journal*, Vol. 17, No. 8.

Rajak, T. (1983) *Josephus*, London.

–––– (1984) 'Was There a Roman Charter for the Jews?', 107–123, in *The Journal of Roman Studies*, Vol. 74.

Ranke-Heinemann, V. (1990) *Eunuchs for the Kingdom of Heaven*, New York.

Rapp, A. (1955) 'The Father of Western Gastronomy', 43–48, in *The Classical Journal*, Vol. 51, No. 1.

Rawson, E. (1969) *The Spartan Tradition in European Thought*, Oxford.

Renehan, R. (1981) 'The Greek Anthropocentric View of Man', 239–259, in *Harvard Studies in Classical Philology*, Volume 85.

Riedweg, C. (2002) *Pythagoras: His Life, Teaching, and Influence*, trans. by Rendall, S., Ithaca, NY and London.

Rives, J. (1995) 'Human Sacrifice among Pagans and Christians', 65–85, in *The Journal of Roman Studies*, Vol. 85.

Rogers, R.S. (1972) *Studies in the reign of Tiberius*, Westport, CT.

Rolfe, J.C. (1904) 'Some References to Seasickness in the Greek and Latin Writers', 192–200, in *The American Journal of Philology*, Vol. 25, No. 2.

Roller, M.B.(2006) *Dining Posture in Ancient Rome*, Princeton, N.J.

Rollier, L.E. 'The Ideology of the Eunuch Priest', 118–135, in Wyke (1998b).

Rose, H.J. (1923) 'Homer's Little Fishes Again', 49–50, in *The Classical Journal*, Vol. 19, No. 1.

–––– (1927) 'Hot Weather in the Classics', 97–105, in *The Classical Review*, Vol. 41, No. 3.

Rosenstein, N. and Morstein-Marx, R. (eds.)(2006) *A Companion to the Roman Republic*, Oxford.

Rosivach, V.J. (1994) *The System of Public Sacrifice in Fourth Century Athens*, Atlanta, GA.

–––– (2006) 'The *Lex Fannia Sumptuaria* of 161 BC', 1–15, in *The Classical Journal*, Vol. 102 / No.1.

Rostovtzeff, M. (1933) 'Hadad and Atargatis at Palmyra', 58–63, in *American Journal of Archaeology*, Vol. 37, No.1.

Ruschenbusch, E. (1966) *Solonos nomoi [The Laws of Solon], die fragmente des solonischen gesetzeswerkes mit einer text und uberlieferungsgeschichte,* Wiesbaden.

Sacks, K. (1981) *Polybius on the writing of history*, Berkeley and London.

Sallares, R (1991) *The Ecology of the Ancient Greek World,* London.

Salomies, O. (ed.)(2001) *The Greek East in the Roman Context: Proceedings of a colloquium organised by the Finnish Institute at Athens, May 21 and 22, 1999*, Helsinki.

Sanders, E.P. (1992) *Judaism: Practice and Belief (63BCE–66CE)*, Philadelphia, PA.

Sauerwein, I. (1970) *Die leges sumptuarie als römische Maßnahme gegen Sittenverfall.* Diss. Hamburg.

Savio, E. (1940) 'Intorno alle leggi suntuarie romane', 174–194, in *Aevum* 14.

Schäfer, P. (1997) *Judeophobia: Attitudes towards the Jews in the Ancient World*, Cambridge, MA.

Scheid, J. (2003) *An Introduction to Roman Religion*, Edinburgh.

Shelton, J. (1988) *As The Romans Did: A Sourcebook in Roman Social History*, Oxford.

Schmidt, W. (1980) 'Effects of Alcohol Consumption on Health', 25–40, in *Journal of Public Health Policy*, Vol. 1, No. 1.

Schnaps, D.M. (2003) 'Socrates and the Socratics: When Wealth Became a Problem', 131–57, in *Classical World* Vol. 96, No. 2.

Schneider, J.W. (1978) 'Deviant Drinking as Disease: Alcoholism as a Social Accomplishment', 361–372, in *Social Problems*, Vol. 25, No. 4.

Scott, J.A. (1917) 'Homeric Heroes and Fish', 328–330, in *The Classical Journal*, Vol. 12, No. 5.

Scott, J.A. (1922) 'The Taboo on Fish in the Worship of the Great Mother', 226, in *The Classical Journal*, Vol. 17, No. 4.

–––– (1923) 'Homeric Heroes and Fish', 242–243, in *The Classical Journal*, Vol. 18, No. 4.

–––– (1936) 'Homeric Heroes and Fish', 171–172, in *The Classical Journal*, Vol. 32, No. 3.

Scott, K. (1929) 'Octavian's Propaganda and Antony's De Sua Ebrietate', 133–141, in *Classical Philology*, Vol. 24, No. 2.

Seaford, R. (1981) 'Dionysiac Drama and the Dionysiac Mysteries', 252–275, in *The Classical Quarterly*, New Series, Vol. 31, No. 2.

–––– (1994) *Reciprocity and Ritual: Homer and Tragedy in the Developing City-State*, Oxford.

Sekora, J. (1977) *Luxury: The Concept in Western Thought, Eden to Smollett*, Baltimore, MA.

Sellars, J. (2006) *Stoicism*, Chesham.

Sheffield, F. (2006) *Plato's Symposium: The Ethics of Desire*, Oxford.

Sigal, P. (1988) *Judaism*, Grand Rapids, MI.

Simoons, F.J. (1978) 'Traditional Use and Avoidance of Foods of Animal Origin: A Culture Historical View', 178–184, in *BioScience*, Vol. 28, No. 3.

Singer, P. (1990) *Animal Liberation*, 2nd edition, London.

Skidmore, C. (1996) *Practical Ethics for Roman Gentlemen: The Work of Valerius Maximus*, Exeter.

Slater, W.J. (1976) 'Symposium at Sea', 161–170, in *Harvard Studies in Classical Philology*, Vol. 80.

–––– (ed.) (1991) *Dining in a Classical Context*, Ann Arbor, MI.

Slingerland, D. (1992) 'Suetonius *Claudius* 25.4, Acts 18, and Paulus Oriosius' *Historiarum Adversum Paganos Libri VII*: Dating the Claudian expulsion(s) of Roman Jews', 12–144, in *The Jewish Quarterly Review*, New Ser., Vol. 83, No.1/2.

Smid, T.C. (1970) "'Tsunamis' in Greek Literature', 100–104, in *Greece & Rome* Vol. 17, No. 1.

Smith Jr., W.S. (1984) 'Horace Directs a Carouse: Epistle 1.19', 255–271, in *Transactions of the American Philological Association (1974)*, Vol. 114.

Sorabji, R. (1993) *Animal Minds & Human Morals: The Origins of the Western Debate*, London.

Sournia, J-C. (1990) *A History of Alcoholism*, Oxford.

Southern, P. (2001) *The Roman Empire from Severus to Constantine*, London.

Spencer, C. (1995) *The Heretic's Feast: A History of Vegetarianism*, Hanover, NH.

Spurr, M.S. (1986) *Agricultural and the 'Georgics'*, 164–187, in *Greece & Rome*, 2nd Ser., Vol. 33, No. 2.

Stern, M. (1976) (ed.) *Greek and Latin Authors on Jews and Judaism*, Volumes 1& 2, Jerusalem.

Stevenson, T. (1998) 'The 'Problem' with Nude Honorific Statuary and Portraits in Late Republican and Augustan Rome', 45–69, in *Greece & Rome*, 2nd Ser., Vol. 45, No. 1.

Stolba, V.F. 'Fish and Money: Numismatic Evidence for Black Sea Fishing', 115–132, in Bekker-Nielsen (2005).

Sutherland, C.H.V. (1974) *Roman Coins*, London.

Syme, R. (1970) *Ten Studies in Tacitus*, Oxford.

Tigerstedt, E.N. (1974) *The legend of Sparta in classical antiquity*, Stockholm.

Toner, J.P. (1995) *Leisure and Ancient Rome,* Cambridge.

Townsend, C.W. (1928) 'Food Prejudices', 65–68, in *The Scientific Monthly*, Vol. 27, No. 1.

Trapp, M. (2007) *Philosophy in the Roman Empire*, Aldershot.

Vandereycken, W. and van Deth, R. (1994) *From Fasting Saints to Anorexic Girls: the History of Self-Starvation*, London.

Vermaseren, M.J. (1977) *Cybele and Attis: The Myth and the Cult*, London.

Vernant, J-P. (1965) *Myth and Thought among the Greeks*, London.

–––– (1991) *Collected Essays*, Princeton, NJ.

Vessey, D.W.T.C. (1971) 'Thoughts on Tacitus' Portrayal of Claudius', 385–409, in *The American Journal of Philology*, Vol. 92, No. 3.

Wacher, J. (1987) *The Roman World*, Volumes I and II, London.

Walbank, F.W. (1972) *Polybius*, Berkeley and London.

Wallace-Hadrill, A. (1983) *Suetonius*, Bristol.

Walzer, R. (1949) *Galen on Jews and Christians*, London.

Ward, A.M. (1974) 'Crassus' Slippery Eel', 185–186, in *The Classical Review*, Vol. 24, No. 2.

Wardman, A. (1976) *Rome's Debt to Greece*, London.

Watson, G.R. (1969) *The Roman Soldier*, Bristol.

Webster, G. (1969) *The Roman Imperial Army of the First and Second Centuries AD*, London.

Weeber, K-W. (2003) *Luxus im alten Rom: Die Schwelgerei, das süsse Gift*, Darmstadt.

Wells, C. (1984) *The Roman Empire (2nd Edition)*, London.

West, M.L. (1969) 'Near Eastern material in Hellenistic and Roman Literature', 113–134, in *Harvard Studies in Classical Philology*, Vol. 73.

White, K.D. 'Cereals, Bread and Milling in the Roman World', 38–43, in Wilkins *et al* (1995).

Whitmarsh, T. (2005) *The Second Sophistic*, Oxford.

Wiedemann, T. (1992) *Emperors and Gladiators*, London and New York.

Wilken, R.L. (1967) 'Judaism in Roman and Christian Society', 313–330, in *The Journal of Religion*, Vol. 47, No. 4.

Wilkins, J. 'Social status and Fish in Greece and Rome', 191–203, in Mars, G., Mars, V. (1993).

–––– (ed.) (1996) *Food in European Literature*, Exeter.

–––– 'Eating in Athenian Comedy', 46–56, in Wilkins (1996).

–––– (2000) *The Boastful Chef*, Oxford.

–––– 'Fish as a Source of Food in Antiquity', 21–30, in Bekker-Nielsen (2005).

Wilkins, J. and Harvey, D. (eds.)(2000) *The Rivals of Aristophanes: Studies in Athenian Old Comedy*, London.

Wilkins, J. and Hill, S. (trans.)(1994) *Archestratus: the life of luxury*, Totnes.

Wilkins, J., Harvey, D., Dobson, M. (eds.) (1995) *Food in Antiquity*, Exeter.

Wilkins, J.M. and Hill, S. (2006) *Food in the Ancient World,* Oxford.

Williams, M. 'Jews and Jewish communities in the Roman empire', 305–333, in Huskinson (2000).

Wright, F.A. (1921) 'Quaestiones Romanae', 155–156, in *The Classical Review*, Vol. 35, No. 7 / 8.

Wyke, M. (ed.) (1998a) *Parchments of Gender*, Oxford.

–––– (ed.) (1998b) *Gender & History: Gender and the Body in the Ancient Mediterranean*, Oxford.

Zeev, M.P.B. (1998) *Jewish Rights in the Roman World: The Greek and Roman Documents Quoted by Josephus Flavius*, Tübingen.

Zuesse, E.M. (1974) 'Taboo and the Divine Order', 482–504, in *Journal of the American Academy of Religion*, Vol. 43.

# INDEX